NO MORE
The formative years of Charles Reeve

© Charles Reeve 2006

All rights reserved

No part of this publication may be reproduced,
stored in a retrieval system, or transmitted
in any form or by any means, without
the prior permission in writing of the publisher,
nor be otherwise circulated in any form of binding or cover
other than that in which it is published and without a similar
condition including this condition being imposed on the
subsequent purchaser.

First published in Great Britain by
Pen Press Publishers Ltd
The Old School
39 Chesham Road
Brighton BN2 1NB

Limited Edition

ISBN: 1-905621-20-5
ISBN13: 978-1-905621-20-0

Printed and bound in the UK

A catalogue record of this book is available from
the British Library

Cover design and setting by Paul Shackcloth

To Frank – A fellow 'sufferer' – and Alma. Happy Reading. Charles.

FOREWORD

At a reunion held in Llandudno for members of the H.M.S. Black Prince Association during the month of April 2001. I had the pleasure of introducing to the members Charles Reeve - the author of the book and also the first Shipmate recruited from H.M.S. Bellona (whose own Association had just been disbanded) to accept the invitation to be enrolled as an Associate Member of the Black Prince Association and who to this date, is still proving to be one of its most reliable and ardent supporters along with his delightful wife Barbara.

It is also with a great deal of pleasure that I have been afforded the opportunity by the author to judge the merits of this book in preparation for its publication. In this task I can confidently affirm to its readers that they are in for a most descriptive introduction into the experiences of a youthful life in the first half of the twentieth century. This period will revive many memories for the older generation and will illuminate for the younger readers the importance of the writer's most formative years in a country not yet recovered from a bitter and deplorable recession and a future filled with the fearful consequences of a second world war. However in between these more serious developments, there is room to reflect on the writer's own development within a family blessed with love and understanding and the determination to overcome the failures of the periods many shortcomings. It also may be true to say, that when compared with today's generation, most of the youth of the earlier part of the twentieth century were accustomed to a strict and disciplined upbringing. Perhaps it was this discipline which drew them closer together and created the comradeship which their generation still remembers with nostalgic pride today.

The author to his credit, also tells the story of his wartime experiences in a style that does not try to debate or expound on the cruelty, destruction or self-sacrifice that transformed the world and left tens of millions dead, but deals truthfully and respectfully with the valuable and significant part played by his shipmates against a formidable and hostile enemy in the dangerous waters of the North Atlantic and in the other operations in which H.M.S. Bellona took part during her full commission with the Royal Navy.

As the earlier chapters of the book unfolded and told their own stories, it soon became clear that the author was proving himself to be a very skilled communicator in all of his domestic, naval and sporting activities. These skills would indeed become paramount in the ambitions he had set for himself in his civilian career, and especially in the very high performance he achieved in the world of Rugby Union on an international stage and in all of his other dedicated sporting challenges.

As well as being a model sportsman who played the game as it should be played, the author is extremely proud to have competed directly in his beloved rugby for a period of over 50 years (akin to another famous sportsman who did the same - Stanley Matthews). His book also records a varied but interesting choice of civilian occupations and traces the development of Charles in the field of entertainment and, which in a distinctive form, is always presented in a professional manner and never fails to induce from the audience the request for "A Little Bit More".

Finally, one must keep the past alive by giving it a place in the future, and Charles has managed to do this with expert knowledge and some subtle humour which shines through all the chapters further enhancing the book into a most enjoyable read. For me, personally however, it also registers a salute to a Brother Shipmate whose experiences bring to mind a few words written by the poet Rupert Brookes which say:

"God I will pack and take the train and get me to England once again
For England's the one place I know. Where men with splendid hearts go"

From a friendly "Signalman" to a very talented "Sparks" - Very best wishes for a worthwhile commission

Bill Edge

DEDICATION

This book is dedicated to all my family to provide them with some insight of my formative years and to those of my shipmates who shared some of them with me.

Charles Reeve, April 2006

ACKNOWLEDGEMENTS

It is perhaps unusual that someone in their eighty first year should attempt to write his first book. I have done so because members of my family and friends who know me well and whose opinions I respect considered that I should describe my early life.

It is a course that I have steered with considerable pleasure and having done so I believe it warrants an attractive presentation. Although the written composition of this work is completely my own, I wish to thank Paul Shackcloth, a good friend and fellow ex rugby player who is also an author in his own right. His practical help and advice during the book's production has been invaluable.

Thanks are also due to Bill Edge for providing the Foreword and my wife Barbara, for her constant support and encouragement throughout the project.

CONTENTS

EARLY DAYS	1
A NOMADIC EXPERIENCE	11
I JOIN THE FRAY	17
THE COLD WAR	27
FAR EAST AND RETURN	54
LETS HAVE A LITTLE BIT MORE	71

EARLY DAYS

The first general strike in British history took place in 1926 and lasted nine days. It was caused by and occurred during a national coal miners strike which was of six months duration. My birth on the 3rd of February of this year was, therefore, no economic triumph for my parents who already had five mouths to feed.

I was the ninth offspring of Robert and Ellen Reeve who both had the misfortune of witnessing the early deaths of five of their children at a very young age which resulted in a huge age gap between the surviving family and myself - the last of the line. However, I was not short of love and in many ways I was spoilt. My sister Doris, ten years my senior, was in effect a second mother to me and I did not hesitate to enrol her assistance on those occasions when it suited me to question my mother's wishes. I understand that the cry of "Look at her Sis!" was often heard from me. My brothers Bill and Arthur, four and two years older than Doris respectively, took me under their wing as and when I became interesting to them and both seemed to enjoy gently introducing me to the world in their own ways.

My father was a foreman fish porter at Billingsgate Fish Market where he worked from 1907 to 1940 when he died of cancer. He was a man with whom I enjoyed a happy and firm relationship, though sadly, a short one. My mother appeared to be a good and dutiful wife and was a kind and caring mother with an essential sense of humour. My earliest memory is of falling on an iron desk in a nursery and cutting my lip which needed stitches. I cried greatly when the time came for their removal despite my mother assuring me that it would not be as painful as their insertion.

I was born at 22 Meeting House Lane, Peckham, S.E. London and from the garden I witnessed the R101 airship passing overhead in 1930 on its way to India. Unfortunately it crashed in France causing Britain to cease production of airships thereafter. Two years later, from the same viewpoint, I also saw the fire at Crystal Palace which lit up the evening sky for miles around, the blaze being visible to pilots crossing the English Channel. Another occasion which shocked football enthusiasts, if nobody else, was the exit of Arsenal from the FA Cup competition in 1932. They lost two nil at the hands of Walsall, a Third Division club at a time when Arsenal were just commencing their run of three successive First Division Championships.

Early childhood was sprinkled with events easy to recall. Following the family's move to the Old Kent Road, I was badly scratched by a pet shop monkey whilst walking to Leo Street School. Later whilst crossing the main road and attempting to avoid a tram, I ran into the back of a lorry. The lorry driver, having kindly escorted me home, seemed to disregard my welfare when he discovered that he knew my father well! I still marvel about the occasion when whilst running along the corrugated roofs of some local multiple garages, I stepped completely through a glass plate window. I fell several feet then continued running on the floor below and through an open door to safety. Fear of apprehension was the driving force. On another occasion I accompanied a group of lads to Greenwich Park, several miles away. I had been given my return fare but spent it on sweets. Whilst in the park I descended a slide in an unconventional manner, toppled over the side and fell to the ground landing head first, grazing my face and breaking a front tooth in the process. The walk home seemed endless, complete with a milk bottle filled with water for gargling.

Marbles was a game widely played, often whilst walking to and from school and along the kerb. 'Tips', 'Spans' and 'Hitsies' was the jargon used. A hit or handspan won the opponent's marble. A hand span which merely tipped the two marbles allowed the thrower to throw again. A game with which I used to amuse myself when alone indoors was to place a chair at each end of a room. These chairs would represent goals and I would designate my left foot Millwall and my right Arsenal and play an imaginary FA Cup Final with a tennis ball. The comics I read were *Champion* and *Radio Fun* rather than the 'twopenny bloods'. These were comics which contained stories of a more violent nature, for example *Hotspur, Wizard* and *Adventure*. The former included the exploits of Rockfist Rogan RAF, a boxer of WW1 vintage who usually contrived to box behind enemy lines. *Radio Fun* was a newly introduced comic which ran a competition amongst its readers requiring them to comment on its stories. My comments were complimentary and suggested that more radio personalities be featured. Twenty prizes of half a crown were awarded and I was fortunate enough to win one.

In 1937 I attained a scholarship to attend Wilsons Grammar School but left shortly afterwards for Walworth Central School where I swiftly learnt about the Rotherhithe Nautical School which I joined in 1938 with a view to joining either the Royal or Merchant Navy. At this period the family were living immediately adjacent to New Cross Stadium which housed Millwall FC.

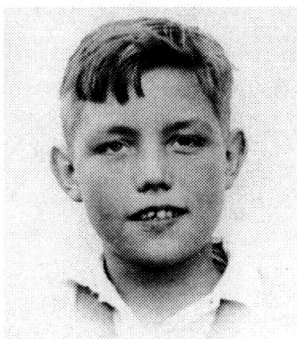

In the playground of Walworth Central School for boys, London SE17, age 12.

(The Den), New Cross Speedway and New Cross Greyhound track. I had the pleasure of watching Millwall become the first Third Division club to reach the FA Cup Semi Final in 1937, beating among others, Manchester City, Chelsea and Derby County (all First Division clubs) and Fulham (Second Division) before being knocked out in the semi final by Sunderland who went on to win the cup.

Entrance to the ground for juniors was gained at the price of sixpence which I acquired by selling buckets of horse manure collected from the local roads during Saturday morning. This was then sold to garden enthusiasts at twopence per bucket. Another sporting attraction was the Speedway where such local heroes as Tom Farndon, Ron Johnson, Jack Milne, George Newton and Stan Greatrex were riding for New Cross. If unable to attend these meetings I would follow proceedings by sitting in my garden and logging the result of each race as it was announced over the tannoy public address system. A further experience was to have my hair cut at Vic's the barbers shop in Canterbury Road which most of the New Cross riders frequented. The conversations overheard were both enlightening and thrilling to an impressionable young lad.

Living so near to the stadium also presented an opportunity to collect brand new cigarette cards from the crowds as they approached the ground and bought cigarettes from the local shops. I would immediately hand them over to brother Bill who would only accept them if they were in pristine condition. Further 'little earners' to the horse manure collection and a paper round was the storing of bicycles used at that time as transport to the grounds by a considerable proportion of the stadium spectators. These were stored on the premises of a cafe situated on the immediate corner of the stadium. It was outside this cafe that I was invited, along with other local young lads, to join members of the New Cross Speedway team and members of the press in a photograph. They were shortly to oppose each other in a cricket match and the picture appeared in a couple of daily newspapers. The accompanying write up referred to we youngsters as lads who had "played the game from the cradle". Amusingly enough many of us had never seen the sky over a cricket pitch! On the publicity side of the football world, an annual event before WW2 at the Den was a challenge match between Jockeys and Boxers. The teams contained many outstanding men of each profession and was usually refereed by a Millwall player. The match was played in a wonderful spirit of jocularity before a capacity crowd - an unlikely scene today, I fear!

My own active sporting pursuits at the time included playing Saturday morning football for Pomeroy Rovers on Peckham Rye and writing my own match reports - particularly if I had scored! My thirteenth birthday present was a new Hercules bicycle which cost 3 pounds 15 shillings on hire purchase. Other possessions were a ball bearing wheeled scooter and a pair of roller skates which cost sixpence per skate from Woolworths who were then advertising 'No articles over sixpence'. Happy days. All these methods of transport were used to represent a locally formed speedway team named 'New Cross' of course. We challenged other teams on a track marked out in the road, would you believe?

I did, however, manage to break away from the speedway environment on my bicycle by taking a camping trip to Weybridge with a friend. We visited Brooklands racetrack which was flourishing nearby and spent a sleepless night near a loud chiming clock because we had pitched the tent in darkness. As a security precaution we tethered our bicycles, which were outside the tent, to our wrists!

Close association with the nearby Long family from Hornshay Place led to their daughters Rose and Phyllis introducing me to Corpus Christi Church where apart from attending Sunday services and becoming confirmed, I became a member of the 14th Deptford Cub and Scout Groups. This provided me with a moderate amount of athletics which I thoroughly enjoyed. In addition to the speedway influence which obviously affected our own local pursuits, two other games were played - either in the road or on the pavement. They were 'Sticks' and a vaulting game called 'Jimmy Nacker'. I do not recall why 'Jimmy Nacker' was so named but when the vaulting side were all seated on the opponents backs, the cry went up 'Hi Jimmy Nacker 1 - 2 - 3, all over, all over' and they became the winners. They were also victorious if the opposition collapsed when 'Weak Horses' were claimed!

The late 1930s were not without attractive holidays for me. Perhaps the most enjoyable was the Scout Camp in Bodmin, Cornwall, made possible by the recent transfer of a Minister from Corpus Christi Church to one in Bodmin. One of these holidays included attending the 'World Scout Jamboree' which was held at Plymouth in 1936 with the rally on Plymouth Argyle Football Ground attended by Lord Baden Powell, founder of the movement. Further scout camps were organised by our troop at Walmer and Dymchurch in Kent. Meanwhile, family holidays were taken to Margate, Ramsgate and Brighton.

During the period between my birth and the outbreak of World War 2, my siblings had developed from being schoolchildren into adults with some years work experience. The senior brother, Bill, joined my father at Billingsgate Fish Market where he was to spend the whole of his working life with the exception of the war years. He attended night school and read intensively with a view to changing his occupation at some stage - but it was not to be.

Brother Bill in his early 20s.

Bill also learned to play chess to a high standard and entered many 'open' competitions which necessitated frequent trips to the homes of landed gentry to play eliminating rounds. Not bad for a lad who, when at home, practised with draught pieces tabulated with chess piece titles because he could not afford the real thing! He also boxed at Deptford Mens Institute and one evening returned home after a bout with some raw meat protruding from under a bandaged eye. (Raw meat contained healing properties for a black eye.) My sister Doris fainted as he walked in. Bill stooped to lift her from the floor and as she came round she opened her eyes to see the raw meat still exposed, and promptly fainted again. Bill was always active and had a lot to do with my mother being confronted with tame mice whenever she went to any of her flower vases. An other instance when Bill organised a ploy to tease my mother occurred one Sunday morning. He and I were both occupying beds in the same bedroom and remaining in them too long to please her. Following repeated threats from downstairs - threats aimed at me as I should have been at church - she decided to mount the staircase, clothes brush in hand, to administer my deserved punishment. Meanwhile Bill, exercising his seniority, suggested that we change beds and hide. The resultant scene was a picture. It captured me smiling broadly whilst Bill, buried beneath the bed clothes in the opposite corner was receiving the punishment destined for me. When he finally emerged laughing loudly, to say to my very exhausted mother "Just what do you think you are doing?" she looked across at me and shamefacedly left the room.

Shove ha'penny was a game which Bill introduced to our household and I was practically weaned on the American boxing magazine 'The Ring' which he took regularly and which published articles on the world boxing hero of the day. Joe Louis was at the time beginning his run of eleven years as undisputed heavyweight champion of the world. I was often taken to watch Bill box at Deptford and he also paid for some of my individual amusements. One little skylark which Bill loved to play with me was 'last touch'. It usually began indoors where we scored against each other frequently and apparently ended when I had left the house with the 'last touch'. On my way to Old Kent Road to catch a tram, from out of nowhere a large hand would be placed on my shoulder and 'last touch' pronounced. I had lost another round and Bill had improved his fitness. Another chase was much more serious. Bill and his girlfriend were kissing on the couch at home when I blew a magnificent raspberry and took off up the road. Bill immediately abandoned his partner and gave chase - but this time I was not caught!

Efforts were made by my father to establish my brother Arthur at Billingsgate but he was unable to withstand hard physical labour, a fact that was aggravated by asthma. With the high level of unemployment prevailing at the time he was therefore without work for long periods which prompted him to join the Royal Air Force as a Flight Rigger shortly before World War Two. I enjoyed many trips to White City with Arthur to watch athletics meetings, also to Herne Hill to watch cycling. One particular memory I have of Arthur is the occasion when he and I together visited my mother, who was then a patient at Miller Hospital, Greenwich. She enquired after Joey, her beloved canary, who unbeknown to her, had been killed by our cat that very day. Arthur's reply was "Oh. He's all right. His cage has never been so tidy", thus delaying the dreaded day when the complete truth would have to be told. Another incident took place during one of his periods of unemployment when his 'job-seeking trousers', as he referred to them, were badly frayed at the bottom. He refused to replace them and my mother finally chased him round the house with the scissors, tearing them so badly that he had to obtain a new pair.

Brother Arthur in Royal Air Force uniform during World War 2.

My sister joined the Milk Marketing Board on leaving school in 1932. She stayed there for as long as she remained single, being employed as a Private Secretary in her final years at the firm. She once bought me a violin and encouraged me to practice - often meeting fierce opposition from my brothers who complained bitterly about the noise. She also paid for my music lessons. One of the many outings she took me on was to the 'New Victoria Cinema' to see Snow White and the Seven Dwarfs. She also took me to visit Uncle Bill and Aunt Nell and Uncle Tom and Aunt Lou in the New Kent Road whose sons together with their father, later travelled daily from Brighton to London working for the press - a journey which seemed monumental to me in those times. Doris returned from one holiday with a diary for me with a Jersey Isle badge attached. I coveted the gift which, to me, took on the proportion of something from a foreign land! During the latter part of the 30s, Doris was under observation for tuberculosis, a research which unfortunately continued for a long period.

My sister Doris, taken in the grounds of Ventnor Hospital, Isle of Wight, 1940

My father was one of identical twin brothers. John, his brother who I never met - possibly because he served with the Army in India - was eventually invalided from the service. I was given to understand that my mother nursed him at some stage on his return from India. He also had a sister, Lil, who married Uncle George. They had two dissimilar twin sons. Dad was as near to being a natural athlete - if such a thing exists - as it is possible to be. He appeared to take no interest in ball sports of any description but he more than once won an event held annually at the Market Sports between Billingsgate, Smithfield and Covent Garden in which the competitors ran carrying one hundredweight of sand on their heads for a mile. The story was told of the occasion when my father celebrated with a few drinks before the event and entertained the spectators with a jig, complete with the sack of sand, before the start of the race which he went on to win. He appeared not to train for this event, but relied on his strength, stamina, and the skill of his trade, locally referred to as 'nutting'. This was the method used to carry multiple boxes etc of fish on the head which was protected by heavy leather headwear.

My father Robert in his early 20s.

Robert enjoying some welcome refreshment with friends

One amusing incident in which my father was involved became a stable joke among our family. In the years leading up to World War Two, my brother Bill joined the Territorial Army. One Sunday morning he was being assisted by my father to don his new uniform prior to a parade. They were both standing in the back garden close to the wall when Arthur - who had spent the previous evening imbibing freely, woke from his slumbers, staggered to the open bedroom window and urinated into the garden. My father, who by now sported a bald patch at the back of his head, touched it saying "It's never raining is it?" He looked upwards as the offending 'weapon' disappeared into Arthur's bedroom. Dad had just placed Bill's bayonet into its sheath. He said to Bill "Give me that bloody bayonet back!" Bill obliged and Dad shot off in pursuit of Arthur. Arthur, who traditionally slept in a shirt, instantly became aware of the danger and sped through the front door to sprint along the road pursued by his angry, bayonet wielding father.

I still treasure fond memories of long walks with my father and also long bus rides to what was then a rural area near Sidcup and then walking for miles. However, following an operation for cancer of the colon, the necessary colostomy limited his activities. Partial recovery enabled him to meet me from school in the afternoon. During this period he was often embarrassed by the possibility of his physical condition giving off an odour, and he questioned me to this effect. I hastened to reassure him that, in fact, his fears were unfounded, and he would continue to enjoy a circuitous stroll home. He was very fond of playing cards and often attended whist drives. When I was quite young he taught me to play German Whist, which necessitated each player holding thirteen cards until the final stage. I must admit that I was able to cheat by being aware of which cards he held by their reflection in his spectacles!

My mother was one of three children. She had a brother Bill and a sister Lou. My Uncle Bill lived at Richmond and had been badly shell-shocked during World War One. In common with many of his comrades he had received little or no legal support when applying for a pension and consequently, no financial support when most needed. Aunt Lou was the wife of Uncle Tom and the mother of two sons, who, with their father, worked for the press. My mother was very homely. She provided all the creature comforts she could under the circumstances and encouraged us to eat well. I accompanied her to two cinema shows per week, usually to the Astoria and Regal, both in Old Kent Road - or maybe the Gaumont, Peckham. I am able to recall seeing only one silent film - "Beau Geste", but remember many early talkies, including 'San Fransisco', 'Dead End', 'Angels with Dirty Faces' and 'The Good Earth'.

My mother Ellen wearing a Royal Air Force brooch during World War Two.

She also introduced me to Music Halls and the entertainers of the time which included Max Miller, Issy Bonn, Nellie Wallace, Arthur Askey, Richard Murdoch and G. H. Elliot. These were to be seen at such venues as the New Cross Empire, Brixton Empress and The Trocadero, Elephant and Castle. She was a mine of information on Music Hall Acts and remembered Dan Leno, a comedian who once held the distinction of being the World Clog Dancing Champion. She cherished visits to her brother, Uncle Bill at Richmond where I played in a large garden with his sons Wilf and Len and Betty his daughter, and to Aunt Lil, her sister-in-law at Bexleyheath. It is unlikely that my mother, whilst enjoying life in the final years of this decade, could foresee that a world war was imminent and that each of her three sons would, in their own way, take part in it. Furthermore that my father would die within a year of its outbreak.

A NOMADIC EXPERIENCE

On September 1st 1939, most of the staff and pupils of Rotherhithe Nautical School, situated in South East London, were evacuated to Hailsham, Sussex. Two days later - on that fateful Sunday - we pupils heard of the declaration of World War 2 announced from a church pulpit, accompanied by the first air raid warning - mercifully a false alarm! This was a war which many of us were not destined to survive. The mobile 'snake', which had wended its way on the Friday, had deposited me, together with two other lads at Home Court, the palatial home of a Mr Green which lacked neither space nor human care. We were well fed - with the many servants in their quarters. The early months of the war saw the introduction of food rationing. We evacuees at Home Court were each allocated our ration of sugar and some other groceries weekly. During the first week I saved my ration of sugar until the last day, but then decided that I could do without it altogether, and have happily done so ever since. We played rounds of putting on the front lawn, roamed the orchard and accompanied Mr Green's brother on long walks through the Sussex countryside. Mr Green, arguably the richest man in Hailsham, owned a large rope factory. Before long we were urgently using this rope to splice rifle pull-throughs for the immediate use of our troops in France. Splicing involved the joining together of two ropes or parts of such by the intertwining of strands.

During the first few weeks of the war, many of us kept personal notebooks in which we entered the name of Merchant Ships sunk by enemy action, together with their registered tonnage, from information being broadcast daily by the BBC. I cannot recall whether this depressing practice was quickly abandoned because of its effect on our morale, or by the BBC for a similar reason nationally. I do recall, however, S.S. Barnhill - an early casualty - lying broken on the beach near Beachy Head to where we cycled to collect tinned food from its holds - until a food poison warning was quickly displayed!

Preoccupied though most of us were in those early days, not all the lads took kindly to their new homes and many were returned from various points on the road to London, where their escape attempts had been frustrated. Meanwhile Lord Haw-Haw had announced (correctly) that a prominent clock in nearby Eastbourne was half an hour slow, and an outbreak of chicken pox meant that two of we evacuees at Home Court entered an isolation hospital. On my discharge I was dispatched to another billet, the home of a Mr King, who was an employee at Mr Green's factory and had been badly gassed during World

War 1.

At this stage my bicycle was sent from London which, among other things, enabled me to deliver newspapers each morning for the local W.H. Smiths. The round was extensive covering a four square mile area and included a delivery at Hellingly Asylum outside whose doors I did not tarry. The billet move was shortly followed by a bigger one. Resulting from the fall of France in June 1940 and the associated fear of invasion, our school was evacuated to two different destinations in South Wales. The senior classes were sent to Ferryside, a fishing village in Carmarthenshire which stood on the River Towy. In many ways this was an ideal base for lads with nautical aspirations. I lived here with one of seven fishing families, the head of which was also coxswain of the local oardriven lifeboat. Random memories include the Biblical touch provided by each crew drawing lots to determine which part of the river they fished, my manning an oar on several fishing trips and the eventual sale of salmon to wholesalers at 2s 6d a pound, and porpoise - whose rapid movement and zig-zag courses often took them through our fishing nets resulting in chaos and unpredictable language from the fishermen.

I also recall the death of my father through cancer in London, whose funeral I was unable to attend, and my foster mother chiding me a "big boy" for sobbing in bed on the night of the funeral. Another but less tragic loss was that of my Hercules roadster bike, somewhere between Hailsham and Ferryside having ostensibly been forwarded by rail. Its arrival would have enhanced my enjoyment of the area - but it was not to be. I had seen the last of my bike so my experiences were necessarily confined to the banks of the Towy - and great they were too! A high tide presented us with a long swim to Llanstephan Castle, a ruin situated on the opposite bank of the river. A low tide afforded an opportunity to catch conger eels which had sheltered in pools beneath rocks when the tide had ebbed. The rocks needed to be prized away with the use of iron bars, and yes - conger eels do bark! Also at low tide the locals were keen that we should be introduced to the joys of rugby, so we played on the Ferryside sand during the evenings. Towards the end of 1940 the opportunity was taken to re-unite the whole school in the town of New Quay in Cardiganshire. Although it was initially necessary to instruct the pupils in two different buildings a quarter of a mile apart, and at first this was considered a temporary measure, the school was destined to remain there for the remainder of hostilities - five years ahead.

New Quay was an even more appropriate home for a nautical school than

Ferryside. It had a coastline on Cardigan Bay and many dozens of retired Merchant Navy Captains, some of whom could be persuaded to spin us a welcome yarn at the drop of a hat. Swimming and boating were available in abundance in what was a natural harbour. Among my lasting memories of New Quay are: Playing rugby, soccer and dancing with the local school age population. Visiting our nearest cinema twenty one miles away in Aberystwyth to see Charlie Chaplin in 'The Great Dictator' and rowing visitors around the bay for a trip in a leaking boat named 'Ruby'. The Liverpool schoolgirl who hid beneath a beached sailing vessel instead of clearing from the beach as advised prior to some rock blasting. Frightened into the open by the explosion, she was killed instantly by a piece of flying shrapnel. Young though we were, we recognised the irony of the circumstance whereby this unfortunate girl, evacuated to avoid explosions had been needlessly killed by one.

At the end of New Quay pier, Cardiganshire, together with six nautical school classmates. The author is second from the right.

The first and most memorable of my New Quay foster mothers was the wife of the engineer of the local fishery protection craft - himself already serving in the Royal Navy. How well she bore the early parting, singing her favourite operatic arias with relish! The acceptance of evacuees by foster parents was not always whole hearted and inevitably, some were more welcoming than others. Not all of them had volunteered and their task was often weighted by the fact that some senior pupils were approaching or had reached sixteen years of age and were beginning to 'feel their feet'. In addition we hailed from London where bombs were already falling and our evacuation area had not experienced one.

At a village two miles along the coast, dances were held - largely for the benefit of a group of non combatant Army Personnel who were stationed there. I can well recall the disparaging parodies we composed about them and sang to the rhythm of various dance tunes played by Mr Fuest, our headmaster, on the piano.

One ran: *"I'm a noncombatant conchie*
             From a non combatant corps
             I'm a non combatant conchie
             I don't want to go to war!" etc

Years on, I'm not at all sure that I fully agree with the sentiments which prompted our attitude towards these men. However we were but ultra patriotic youths, which naturally befitted a group destined for the high seas before very long. Overall, we fitted in well with the local population and friendships blossomed to the extent that several ex-pupils - myself included - have visited New Quay during the post war years and a few married girls from the town. There was generally a relaxed atmosphere, with regular school dances and plenty of swimming available in the harbour during summer time. Our school syllabus was designed to prepare pupils, theoretically, for the standard of a Second Mates Examination in the Merchant Navy, though the only uniform available to the school was that of the Royal Navy with a nautical school cap ribbon. Nautical subjects taught were Navigation, Chartwork, Seamanship, Meteorology and Ship Construction together with Morse and Semaphore Signalling and Boatwork. In London the latter involved marching to Surrey Commercial Docks with our own oars prior to evacuation and rowing around the dock in a leaky old boat. This activity improved beyond all recognition in New Quay where sound craft were available to us.

All these subjects were taught by Captain Harvey who had served as an Extra Master Mariner in the Merchant Navy. He was a Cornishman with a strong resonant voice and a character which endeared him to us all. Although we may not have realised it at the time, he was an expert at driving a point home by firstly making it to the whole class and then asking a lad at random to answer a question on it. The chosen pupil would stand to answer - the custom at the time - until his answer revealed that he had not fully understood it. "Sit down Muggins!" would be Captain Harvey's loud retort, followed by him repeating word for word his original statement. It is a tribute to him that sixty or more years on, many of us, I am sure, are still able to repeat several cogent points that he made - in a multitude of subjects. It was, of course, not unknown for the lad answering the question to deliberately answer wrongly, knowing that the usual procedure would follow. How we all loved it - and so I suspect did he!

One subject was the reading of morse code transmitted on a loud buzzer by the Captain. He was a lover of the works of Rudyard Kipling and invariably used a passage from one of his poems as the subject matter of a text message. Some attempted to 'pull a fast one' by learning some of Kipling's poems in order that once the first word of the message had been received, they were able to guess the remainder rather than read it. Although deceitful in some ways, this practice illustrated that the poems of Kipling were attractive to most of us - either then or later.

As part of the national 'Dig for Victory' campaign, the senior class was encouraged to develop and maintain vegetable allotments in the field adjacent to the local church. This required a skill which none of us had practised before. Meanwhile Sunday afternoons were sometimes spent walking to Aberayron - seven miles along the coast and home of the County School which many of the local boys and girls attended daily. Each Nautical School pupil needed to decide which Navy he wished to join before he reached the age of sixteen. If the Merchant Navy was his choice, a premium would need to be paid to the appropriate shipping company and the Apprentice Officer uniform and kit required would cost approximately forty pounds. Given the recommendation of Captain Harvey, the premium would be waived, leaving the uniform and kit only to be paid for by the apprentice. Entry to the Royal Navy was free and was dependent upon a medical and written examination which would determine which branch of the service would be open to the applicant.

Whilst my preference was for the Merchant Navy, particularly as our training had been designed to this end, it was, nevertheless, clearly impossible for me to raise forty pounds (this amount constituted approximately fourteen weeks of a working man's average salary) as my mother was widowed. An alternative might have been to leave school immediately, earn the necessary sum quickly in a London munitions factory and then join the Merchant Navy. However I feared that earning such a sum so early in life would dissuade me from going to sea, which I wanted to do above all else. Consequently I opted for the Royal Navy.

Early in 1942 I was summoned to Bristol Royal Navy Recruiting Centre to be examined for entry into the Royal Navy as a Boy for twelve years service commencing at the age of eighteen. I passed the medical examination and qualified for the Communications Branch educationally - which was the most elevated branch available to boy entrants at the time. A notable feature of recruitment was the high physical standard that the Royal Navy required of their permanent service recruits. Despite the obvious and urgent need of recruitment during these war years, I was the only successful applicant of seven that afternoon. The most common reason for failure being insufficient or poor teeth, along with colour blindness and general optic deficiency. The mother of one disappointed lad who had accompanied him to the recruiting centre, kindly took me to a theatre performance that evening.

Following my return to New Quay, it was only a question of time, very little time, before I received my call up papers - to report to H.M.S. St. George at Douglas, Isle of Man. During this waiting period, Desmond Doyle (a pupil and friend waiting to join the Eagle Oil Company) and myself attended few lessons and in general had an opportunity to reflect on our time as evacuees. In my case I had been evacuated for a relatively short time but had nevertheless lived in three different towns and seven different dwellings. During this period my mother, now living in Walworth, was bombed out of her home, which of course meant me staying at yet another new address when on leave.

Other changes - with world wide repercussions - had taken place since the outbreak of war. The occupation of Poland by Germany and Russia had been completed. H.M.S. Royal Oak had been sunk at anchor in Scapa Flow following the surprise penetration of its defenses by a German U-boat. Russian forces had occupied Finland. Germany had intensively bombed Denmark, Holland, Belgium and Norway before finally occupying them. Winston Churchill had succeeded Neville Chamberlain as Prime Minister of Great Britain and the Allied Forces had evacuated from Dunkirk. Britain now stood alone. Following Dunkirk, Italy joined Germany as an Axis Power and invaded France. The Channel Islands were occupied by Germany and the Battle of Britain in the air began with Germany hoping to follow this up with their invasion. This was prevented - but not without a magnificent defence by the Royal Air Force, the courage which was evident in many cities, including London and Coventry and the fact that Hitler respected our navy sufficiently to avoid an attempt to cross the sea with an invasion force before establishing air superiority.

Yugoslavia had also been occupied by Germany. H.M.S. Hood and the German Battleship Bismark had been sunk. Germany had broken its non-aggression pact with Soviet Russia by invading them. The American fleet at Pearl Harbour had been bombed by Japanese planes thereby bringing the United States into the war as our ally and Japan as our enemy.

I JOIN THE FRAY

When I joined the Royal Navy the Admiralty was intensifying its recruiting campaign. Entry to its Boy Service was open to boys who were medically and educationally acceptable and of good character from the age of 15 years 3 months to 16 years 6 months. Recruitment was aimed at the ex-civilian work force, ex schoolboys and ex training ship boys. Most of them were keen to join a fighting service during a World War. The engagement was for twelve years of mans service which commenced at 18.

The boys training establishment was H.M.S. St George, a 'stone wall frigate', situated in Douglas, Isle of Man. My sea trip to Douglas from Fleetwood was eventful in many ways. To begin with, the assortment of individuals with very different backgrounds who assembled aboard the S.S. Rushen Castle were meeting for the first time. Secondly the weather for the crossing was rough, probably rougher than any of us had experienced in our short lives to date. Thirdly - many of the group had already smoked - a habit which would be abandoned on arrival at *St. George!* This trip therefore, was regarded by them as a 'swansong' and many of the non-smokers, myself included, gave them every assistance in consuming their remaining stock - often with disastrous results!

Although I was not physically sick on the crossing, I spent the first hours of my naval career in a long sick bay queue seeking treatment for the gastro enteritis which I had developed. Whilst waiting I needed to pay a hasty visit to the toilet where the agonising decision had to be made as to which part of my body should be allowed to leave a deposit on the deck - a case of urgent and simultaneous motivation of course. Having made my decision I sat on the seat provided and very nervously reported to somebody who appeared to be in a position of authority and offered to clean it up. I was informed that I should stop making a fuss and get back in the queue. This I did. Imagine my surprise when the comparative silence was broken by a Petty Officer shouting loudly "Who's made this bloody mess here? Some of you think you're on your father's yacht". The shape of things to come. I spent the next two days or so in the sick bay ward and then rejoined the main intake of new entries.

As things began to take shape it became evident that the New Entry Division, which we were to adorn for six weeks was to become quite an eye opener. Known as 'nozzers' to the remainder of the inmates, we were kept apart from them, whilst for their part they were either receiving their appropriate academic and technical instruction or had completed it and were in Draft Division awaiting posting to their first ship. In preparation for what lay ahead, we received our first service haircut, were given medical and dental examinations and other necessary treatment. We were made aware of all behavioural restrictions and punishable offences. It was made abundantly clear that all naval personnel, other than boys within the establishment, were to be addressed as 'Sir'. This applied to instructors whatever their rank and included Leading Seamen. It was necessary to embroider one's name into each article of kit immediately, with the exception of the oilskin and the hammock. This amounted to approximately sixty items. How grateful I was that my surname was REEVE rather than to share the fate of my divisional colleagues LITTLEWOOD, WINTERBOTTOM and FITZCLARENCE.

All new entries were 'Boys 2nd Class' and paid five shillings and threepence per week of which each boy received one shilling on the top of his cap held in his hand and presented to the Paymaster after enduring the boredom of a lengthy queue. Before payment was made he also had to quote his Ship's Book Number and woe betide him if it was decreed that he had not spoken loudly and clearly - he would be made to retreat to the rear of the drill shed and shout his Ship's Book Number repeatedly followed by the obligatory "Sir" until told 'enough', when he would finally receive his pay. The remainder of this pay was accumulated throughout his training period and credited to him when he finally left *St. George* for his first ship.

Many things available to civilians of his age were denied the Boy Seaman. He was forbidden to have long hair, wear any form of jewellery, including a watch or any item of non-service origin, possess more than two shillings and sixpence in cash, be tattooed or smoke until Captain Halsey, a humane character successfully championed the right to smoke for boys, some of whom were well above civilian smoking age. One of the most common offences for which a boy could receive '12 cuts' applied to the buttocks with a heavy cane weilded by a hated Regulating Petty Officer, was smoking. It was even possible to be transferred to a Military Prison at Preston if the offence was repeated often enough by any boy.

In addition to boys being looked down upon and often harshly treated by Senior Naval Personnel, certain civilians in firmly established posts at *St. George* delighted in giving the lads an unjustifiably rough time. Among this number were the tailor, the canteen supervisor and the barber. The ordeal of abandoning civilian clothing for full naval kit was to some, painful enough without a tailor enjoying his position of power by making such remarks as "You don't need a cap lad, you need the box they came in!" and behaving as if it was beneath them to assist boys, who after all, had volunteered at a very young age to serve their country.

A class mate of mine, Tony Culley, was seen to walk in an ungainly manner which earned him the nickname 'kipperfeet', to which his response was "It's not my feet mate - it's my boots!" This was true of course. Tony was a type, often encountered in life, who was academically bright but possessed little common sense. Whilst drawing our issue of kit, he was standing next to a far-seeing colleague who decided to ask for a size larger in boots than usual in anticipation of the square bashing which lay ahead. He therefore asked for size 11, a move which Tony considered wise. He therefore 'fell in line' by asking for size 11 himself, completely overlooking the fact that he normally wore size 8!

The Canteen Supervisor was a most unpleasant character who was happiest when severely rationing any delights available and revelled in encouraging long queues of boys to wait to be served and closing the canteen long before they were. The scene in the barber's shop when new entries were receiving their first naval haircut was often chaotic with some boys attempting to assault the barber who had rid them of their coveted locks - only to be marched away to receive harsh punishment.

From the outset it became clear that the levels of oppression set by the Instructors and condoned by the Officers were met with varying response. The boys from training ships were younger than the remainder with only a faint idea of life outside their orphanages, therefore familiar with an institutional way of life and less critical of circumstances. The boys who had enlisted from normal civilian life, however, included those who had experienced employment and those who had remained at school until the age of sixteen.

Despite the initial difference in response to oppression by these two groups, they began to merge into an identical group which fought a battle of subterfuge with the Instructors but when they were defeated the penalty was severe. The most feared forms of punishment were '12 cuts' and 'jankers', a military slang term - the latter of which caused defaulters to be double

On the parade ground at H.M.S. St George.

marched on the parade ground for one hour daily with a rifle held aloft. At the conclusion of 'Nozzer' period, all boys were transferred to classes within Divisions sporting such names as Anson, Bembow, Drake, Frobisher, Hawke and Exmouth. The necessary segregation was in accordance with ability and choice and the Branch options were Communications or Seaman Branch, the latter being divided into Advanced and General Class. The Seaman (G) course was of 26 weeks duration, Seaman (A) 36 weeks and Communications 52 weeks. My choice was Communications with Wireless Telegraphy in mind and I became a member of Anson 243 Class under the supervision of a Chief Petty Officer Telegraphist and a Chief Yeoman of Signals.

All boys in the class were given comprehensive communications training for the first twelve weeks before being divided into Wireless Telegraphy (W/T) or Visual Signalling (V/S). In addition an academic course was commenced which, inter alia, determined whether one was Commissioned Officer material. I managed to keep abreast of both the technical and academic courses without much trouble as in many ways it was a continuation of the schooling which I had already received. In other ways it was revision, for I could read morse by buzzer and lamp at 12 words per minute, and semaphore on leaving the Nautical School. There were ways to fall by the wayside and be 'dipped' to a lower class. These included requiring 'backward buzzer', 'backward flashing' and extra school work or spending a long period in sick bay. Another hazard, although not one involving 'dipping' to a lower class was requiring 'backward swimming' lessons because before being allowed to join his first ship, each boy had to pass a check test personally attended by the Commander of the establishment. This included swimming one hundred yards in a canvas duck suit and inflating a life-belt whilst treading water.

One incident in this respect which was welcomed by the boys in their battle against authority occurred when Commander's Check Tests were taking place in the swimming pool. With the Commander assuming his usual position - seated on his shooting stick at the 'lifebelt' end of the bath - one lad, having exhausted himself swimming the required distance was having no success with inflating his lifebelt. The Commander impatiently stood, leant over the bath side and shouted "You are not trying boy!" meanwhile extending his stick in an effort to prod him. Determined to 'get his retaliation in first', the lad clutched the stick thereby pulling the Commander headlong into the water. The sight of the Commander in a completely new uniform at Divisions next morning, was greeted with glee by 1,500 boys, all of whom had heard the joyous news on the 'grapevine'. The protagonist, however, was not seen again for some time!

A constant background to life at *St. George* was compulsory sport. It was compulsory for all boys to play such sports as rugby, soccer, cricket, athletics, boxing, gymnastics and rifle shooting. To those of us who had already participated in sport this was not too much of a shock but for some it was little short of catastrophic. The ultimate sufferers, however, were not invariably those who had not previously participated. Those who had not hitherto played rugby were completely ignorant of the laws of the game. They therefore, naturally recognised one law only - that of the jungle - self preservation, which meant that they used any means available to inflict punishment on others and thereby survive themselves! For us well informed players, the results bordered on the gruesome.

One memory of a cheeky action on the rugby pitch refuses to go away. It is of the Establishment Final between Anson Division (my own) and Exmouth which was played before a huge crowd including officers and their wives who sat in relative comfort near the touch lines. I was a member of the Anson XV which included George Figgett who had played good rugby at school and was the team's kicker. He was poised to attempt a conversion following a try having been scored. As he prepared for the kick the Exmouth team prematurely advanced from their goal line and the charge was disallowed. In his merriment, George made a V sign, enthusiastically, to the opposition - at which our Divisional Officer who sat nearby, exclaimed "Good God - Figgett" and almost fell from his shooting stick. Other high ranking officers were similarly affected - but this did not prevent George from kicking the goal.

Meanwhile in boxing I was matched initially with a boy of my own height (weight seemed to be of no importance). My opponent was quite heavy and because of inexperience and lack of interest, was virtually unable to defend himself. He was no match for me as I had moderate boxing experience. I therefore very quickly tired of hitting him at will and thereby incurred the displeasure of the Petty Officer Physical Training Instructor who immediately placed me in Commander's Defaulters and provided me with more worthy opposition from a class boxing elsewhere in the gymnasium. It took the shape of last year's beaten finalist in the Establishment Middleweight Division. What a set to we had!

The lad who started it all, Costigan, my original opponent and classmate, was forever goaded by our P.T.I. for being a coward. He did this on one occasion when he was unable to 'make fast' on climbing a single rope. This consisted of climbing half way up the rope and releasing the grip with the hands whilst maintaining one's position on the rope with the feet. Costigan invariably came sliding down the rope at this stage. It always impressed me as ridiculous that he should be labelled a coward yet selected from 1,500 boys as full back for the *St. George* rugby XV, a position from which he never funked a tackle!

Sport was regarded quite highly by the Commissioned Officers and for a boy was the only avenue to a prize of two shillings and sixpence and a 9pm shore leave (rather than the usual 6pm shore leave which only allowed for one cinema visit). It therefore became something of a status symbol and was made possible by representing your class in one of the many sports competitions and becoming ship's champions. Our class won the cricket competition which, to me, meant the prize and two cinema shows in one afternoon and evening. One film showing was Noel Coward in "In which we serve". It was the story of a British destroyer which was sunk by enemy action and contained a scene where the survivors are clinging to a raft as yet again German planes return to attack them. One of the survivors, quite naturally, said "Here the bastards come again!" This sentence fell upon a largely stunned and surprised audience - this was 1941!

It was at *St. George* that I witnessed my first and last milling competition. Milling was similar to boxing containing most of its laws but with a distinct difference. It took place in the boxing ring with the participants wearing boxing gloves. One team of eleven - all different weights - opposed another similar team and each bout was of only one minute duration following the previous one commencing simultaneously with its conclusion. Each team's competitors queued immediately outside the ring awaiting their own starting bell. The competition was short and swift and the whole proceeding was a flurry of gloves and bodies. The winners came from the perpetual motion hitters. There was no time or opportunity in one minute to box as such. Knockouts were common as were eleven - nil results, not necessarily because one team was particularly superior man for man but because the sight of their predecessors being unmercifully subdued was too much for some lads and they were beaten before they stepped in the ring. It was suspected that money changed hands among the officers in this sport as in many others.

Daily life tended to become routine but there was always the odd occasion to raise the eyebrow. One occurred when an officer was found guilty of indecently assaulting a boy and another when a lad from Eire, one of many who had overstayed their long leave, and who had returned together, struck the Captain after being awarded his punishment. We saw nothing of this boy for a period as he was serving a sentence in Preston Services Jail on the mainland. Meanwhile, however, his colleagues after collecting their quota of 'cuts', were seen on the parade ground doing 'jankers' for many a week - much to the chagrin of the other defaulters. The reason being that the Irish lads muttered continuously whilst drilling which infuriated the Gunner's Mate in charge who therefore kept everybody at the double, often with the rifle above the head. They were not popular. I recall betting (quite illegally of course) a group of some twenty lads from Ireland sixpence a piece that Field Marshal Montgomery was born in Kennington, London and not in Ireland as they insisted. Long arguments evolved, but eventually it was agreed that a national newspaper should arbitrate. Meanwhile I was aware that the colossal debt that I would incur, should I be incorrect, may well affect my future enjoyment of life. In the event I won the bet, and more importantly they all paid up!

Another occurrence which had a devastating affect on me was my habit, along with others, to take short cuts across farmers' fields - enjoying raw vegetables en-route, and thereby occupy a flattering position at the finishing post of class cross country races. This of course resulted in many of us representing our division in the establishment finals, but not on merit. It soon became evident that the lads of the other divisions had not been so wayward and a surprisingly large number of Anson Division were struggling in a battle to be last! Retribution was mild in this case and simply took the form firstly of sentries being posted at various parts of the finals course and consequently the pain of having to run the full distance for the very first time.

Such was not the case on another jaunt which I indulged in towards the end of my time at *St. George* when the punishment was more severe. One evening after 'lights out' I decided to 'break ship' and sample the night life of Douglas. The outing was a success during which I met up with several lads from other divisions on a similar mission. We enjoyed a little freedom, a hearty meal and a couple of beers and each of us made the final part of the return trip alone. Crossing the sports fields which surrounded our quarters was without incident but as I mounted the steps to my chalet, which I shared with two other lads, a torch was switched on from my bunk area where sat an R.P.O. to welcome me aboard. The outcome of it all was six 'cuts' and fourteen days 'jankers'. However I must have spun a plausible yarn to the Commander for I gathered later that the other defaulters received twelve 'cuts' each.

Eventually, the transfer to Draft Division took place and the first task for each boy in the class was to complete a Will, which, at the time, struck many of us as a joke, but its serious side was soon emphasised by the news of whole or part classes being killed after joining some of the larger battleships eg: H.M.S. Hood. With the necessary academic, technical and physical qualifications behind us and the dreaded Commander's swim check test completed the only remaining obstacle was the laying of kits in the gymnasium. This was the ritual of laying kits consisting of above sixty items, all of which needed to be rolled with the owner's name on display and tied with clothes stops a precise distance apart. It is astonishing to recall what a blow it was for any boy to experience the disappointment of being told that he was unready for sea for one or more of the many reasons that could bring about this decision. The delay in a boy being considered ready for his first ship often meant a temporary lease of life, but nobody considered this and each strove for perfection. On completion of training, large drafts of boys were sent to battleships and cruisers and many of these ships were being sunk with few survivors, eg H.M.S. Hood.

The establishment *St. George,* which we would soon be leaving, had previously been and would later revert to being Cunningham's Holiday Camp. It consisted of lower and upper section linked by a tunnel which had been built by German prisoners of war during World War One. At the bottom end of the tunnel was our quarterdeck. Although the Admiralty held great sway in the area, it was believed that a rostrum which was used to mark the finishing line of the Tourist Trophy Race held in the Isle of Man before the war and situated on our playing field was left in place at the request of the local authority and remained so until the end of hostilities. *St. George* was established during the early months of the war in order to facilitate the evacuation of H.M.S. Ganges. the previous boys training establishment at Shotley on the Suffolk coast. The aim was to continue the training of those boys who had commenced their courses at *Ganges* and admit further recruits during hostilities.

Imagine the surprise and delight of the first arrivals when they entered *St George* to be greeted with waitress service in the dining hall rather than the austere routine which they had been accustomed to at *Ganges*. This was because the holiday camp staff had not yet been withdrawn. The Admiralty swiftly remedied this situation - henceforth the dining hall accommodated all 1,500 boys at one sitting. They were divided into messes of 20 and sub standard food was drawn from the galley by two boys from each mess who allocated and distributed it at the mess table. The entire meal period was supervised by several Chief Petty Officers. Before eating commenced a commissioned officer enquired publicly "Is there any boy without a meal?" and "Are there any spare meals?" followed by a short grace. I cannot recall any spare meals being reported.

Doris and Fred's wedding attended by (left to right) Tom Ward, Brother Arthur, Uncle George and Grace. My mother and Aunt Lil are in the foreground.

When I left for my first ship there were several ex-nautical schoolboys following their respective courses. During my time there, my sister Doris had married Fred, a policeman, and brother Bill had married Rose, an officer in the Auxiliary Fire Service. One of my leaves had been spent in Pewsey, Wiltshire, visiting my mother, who together with her sister Lou, had evacuated from London - my mother having been yet again 'bombed out'. Several of us were sleeping in a farm loft with light curtains as screens. My return trip which included a bus accident on my way to catch a train at Swindon, almost resulted in my reporting back adrift.

On the battlefront, the World War had continued to spread to an even greater number of areas. We were now fighting against Germany and Italy in the Middle East. The Japanese had taken Singapore and Hong Kong. The RAF had commenced large scale bombing raids on Lubeck and Cologne. The St. Nazaire and Dieppe raids had taken place and the naval Battle of Midway had been fought. Inevitably the day arrived when a group of lads, each either Wireless Telegraphists or Visual Signalmen left Douglas for an unknown destination. Only now were we able to claim the money which we had accumulated as the residue of our weekly payment entitlement, before setting out on a journey which was to end with the commencement of our sea going careers.

It took us across the Irish Sea to Fleetwood, then via Preston Station with its free serviceman's canteen facility, to Thurso on the northern tip of Scotland. Despite all necessary security measures it was now quite obvious to us all that we were bound for the desolation of Scapa Flow, base of the home fleet. We were now a ferry trip away from H.M.S. Bellona, a newly built light cruiser which was to be our home until hostilities with Germany ceased.

THE COLD WAR

H.M.S. Bellona was built in Fairfields Yard at Govan in 1943. Her class which included *Black Prince, Diadem, Royalist* and *Spartan* was intended to be a modification of the Dido class. Her armament consisted of eight 5.25 inch guns (main), twelve 2 pounder Anti Aircraft guns, twelve 20mm Anti Aircraft guns and six 21 inch torpedo tubes. She had a speed of 32 knots and a complement of five hundred and thirty. Our group joined her a few weeks after she had been commissioned and we completed the complement of her Communications Branch.

Many of the 'Sparkers' (Wireless Telegraphists) and 'Bunting Tossers' (Visual Signalmen) were from a class that left *St. George* only a matter of weeks before us. Among my group were Tony Culley and 'Lofty' Desmond Blackwell, a former classmate at the Nautical School. We three were 'Sparkers'. Joining *Bellona* at Scapa Flow involved being introduced to an austere monastic life with wretched weather. A run ashore was an extremely bleak experience without female company of any sort and completely void of domestic comfort, though, strangely enough, we were destined to visit a far less attractive port before too long.

H.M.S. Bellona anchored off Rosyth.

Once fully manned, *Bellona* carried out working-up trials in the Pentland Firth, at most times one of the roughest waterways in the world. Working-up trials involved testing the ship against all the possibilities and tribulations likely to come her way during her hopefully long life. When the time came our crew was certain that the Captain's main aim was to discover how long the ship could steam upside down. Many of the crew who were on these trials for the first time found weather conditions, the firing of a complete gunnery broadside and various simultaneous manouvres quite precarious and wondered what would happen next. On reflection it is no surprise to me that the only area in which I was ever seasick, during my long service in the Royal Navy was not the Bay of Biscay, the Irish Sea, on the Murmansk run or in a typhoon - but in the Pentland Firth during these working-up trials. Every part of ship and ship's company were thoroughly tested physically and mentally, but in keeping with most experiences it was not completely without its humorous side. One of the gunnery exercises required us to fire at a target towed by a plane, the target being an appreciable distance astern of it. During the 'shoot' an anxious voice was heard on our R/T receiver "Hey, you down there. I'm pulling this bloody target not pushing it!" So much for the pilot's evaluation of our gunnery.

Completion of our working-up trials and the subsequent period in harbour at Flotta provided an opportunity for we new crew members to acclimatise ourselves aboard ship. In many ways this was an awesome task. We soon discovered that at seventeen plus we were at the very lowest end of the age scale. There were men aboard who had been at Jutland and the Dardanelles in World War One and pensioners who had been recalled for wartime service, many of them well into their fifties. Some were grandfathers and had certainly not envisaged serving in another war.

Here then was a war-time crew, numerically well in excess of the ship's peace-time complement consisting of personnel from different backgrounds and from most areas of Britain with accents accordingly. All these were expected to quickly blend into an effective fighting unit. Whether we liked it or not we were expected to serve aboard this ship together with a group whose company we had not chosen and with whom we might have little in common. This ship with strictly limited space was to be our home - seldom upright, seldom stable and very seldom still. It was also to be our club, our church, our only fairway and on very rare occasions, our cinema. We were to eat and sleep in precisely the same area and when necessary, use doorless lavatories. Any form of privacy was a thing of the past.

Our group's welcome aboard consisted of being escorted to our tempo communications messes, allotted a hammock billet, allocated an Act. Station and taken to the C.C.O. (Central Communications Office) where th telegraphists amongst us would spend much of our time. Whether I was on watch or not the frequent sound of the 'Action Stations' alarm would, in future, send me scurrying downwards through at least two narrow hatchways to my station as the only telegraphist in the Gunnery Transmitting Station. I was convinced that our Chief Petty Officer Telegraphist exercised his sense of humour by selecting one of his heaviest men to squeeze through these minute hatchways to keep the company of 'Bootnecks' - our term of endearment for Royal Marines.

Since we were the last group to join the ship's crew, there were no lockers available in which to stow smaller items of our kit. I had to keep my effects entirely in a kit bag - or not to do so and endure the ignominy of having to retrieve any item 'left loafing', from the scran bag (a secure area where abandoned kit was placed by the Leading Hand of the Mess) - at a later date and at a price. When many months later I managed to procure a locker it was far from my mess, below decks and at deck level which resulted in cherished books, magazines and other modest possessions being ruined by the ever present sea water which attacked everything and everybody.

Shortly after I first stepped aboard *Bellona*, I went to the Regulation Petty Officer in an effort to start proceedings to reverse a decision which had been made at *St. George* following an eye test which I had considered untimely. It had followed my reporting to Sick Bay complaining of an eye which was often watering. After the test the authorities deemed that I was not fit to commence a twelve year period at the age of eighteen as a telegraphist. I was therefore given the choice of transferring to serve as a Short Service Telegraphist for seven years followed by five years on the reserve or to one of various other branches for twelve years. Having already completed part of my Telegraphy course I chose the former. This episode left me feeling something of a failure and I wished to revert to a twelve year serving Telegraphist if at all possible. I said as much to the Regulating Petty Officer who laughed loudly and said "Don't be a bloody fool son. See me in a year's time and we'll see how you feel then!"

As life unfolded aboard the ship I began to realise that I had perhaps allowed pride to cause me to act hastily in this matter. After all, one advantage of being Short Service was that I received Ordinary Telegraphist pay - instead of that of a boy from seventeen and a half years, and indeed was doing so before joining *Bellona*. The remainder of my group were to wait for their eighteenth birthdays before doing so. Comparatively, this made me a 'baron'. Added to which, although I was happy enough with life, this feeling might not last. Perhaps the R.P.O. was right after all!

During this short stay at Scapa Flow, the ship landed a rugby team to play the cruiser *Uganda* which was manned by Canadians. I played in the front row of the scrum with the Ship's Padre in the second row. The match, which resulted in a rare score - nil all - was played on a pitch whose dimensions were reduced because of the muddy state of the ground. We had yet to learn that the poor state of the pitches would be a regular feature at whatever time of year games were played, but any form of recreation was a welcome gift under the circumstances. The ship spent its first Christmas following commission at Scapa Flow and on Boxing Day the German Battleship *Scharnhorst* was sunk by a force led by H.M.S. Duke of York following the German attempt to intercept Convoy JW55B on its way to Murmansk - perhaps the only cause for us to cheer during an otherwise bleak Yuletide. We were probably one of the very few ships based at Flotta not involved in this action. Early the following year *Bellona* left for Plymouth where she was based for various operations in the Western Channel and off North West France. We were now in somewhat warmer waters and a run ashore in Plymouth was far removed in more ways than one from a trip ashore at Scapa Flow.

In April '44 *Bellona* was allocated for the Normandy invasion 'Operation Neptune' as a bombarding ship in the Western Task Force (US Navy). During this period I took the opportunity to sit my Telegraphist examination at Devonport Signal School and a few weeks later passed for Telegraphist (Trained Operator) - both minor promotions resulting in an equally minor rise in pay. The Normandy landings were preceded by patrols in the Bay of Biscay together with exercises and preparations for D Day which was originally scheduled for 5th June but because of rough weather postponed for twenty four hours. *Bellona,* together with ships of many different allied Navies was berthed off Belfast waiting for the 'Off' and during this time the personnel of all fleets were, once, allowed ashore together - but never again! The blend of Nationalities together with the Irish already ashore was explosive, the result being that a rota was quickly established whereby the servicemen of each nationality went ashore on different days. Unfortunately for me I had been briefed (as a supervisor of a W/T watch) for the forthcoming operation and was not allowed ashore at Belfast at all. Pleasure deferred!

An amusing communications incident occurred during a Wireless Middle Watch (Midnight - 4am). Since we were all in harbour there was very little traffic on Radio Telephony. An operator on an American ship monotonously and repeatedly checked his strength of signals with the same British ship and on each occasion the message ran 'A, this is B. How do you hear me. Over'. The optimum reply would be 'Hearing you 5 by 5' which indicates good strength and modulation. However, the British operator, now completely threadbare with the whole proceedings replied 'B, this is A. Hearing you 2 by 2. Too loud and too bloody often!' This breach of discipline was, of course, followed by a 'witch hunt' from the Senior Officer of the British force, but in the event, since more important things were imminent, no heads rolled.

On 5th June, the day of the decision to defer the operation by a day, our force was half way between Belfast and France already which meant that we had to return towards Belfast and occupy the same positions at the same time the following day. Many of the ships taking part were, of course, already lying off the south coast. As we rounded the south coast we rendezvoused with several ships of the American Task Force under the command of Admiral Bryant aboard U.S.S. Texas. The scene was amazing and it was the only time in my career at sea that there appeared to be more ships than water. Over five thousand ships and craft were to take part in Operation 'Neptune', the nautical component of Operation 'Overlord'. During the landing of the troops on Omaha Beach, Admiral Bryant himself aboard *Texas* used the radio telephones to issue instructions and each ship's R/T set was manned by its Captain.

Although 6th June was finally chosen as D Day because of rough weather on the 5th, conditions were still not ideal for landing troops. However it was considered to be the only remaining day for some time which would provide suitable tides etc. The progress of troops landing on and clearing Omaha Beach was slower and more problematical than that of all the other beachheads and at times seemed doomed to failure. The Germans held a defensive position which was naturally strong and elaborately fortified. Rows of objects planted below the high water level were covered by anti-tank guns. Mines and barbed wire were positioned in the shallow water and on the beaches. Exits were also mined.

Prior to Operation Overlord the British planners had offered the Americans equipment to deal with these beach obstacles but they preferred straight forward frontal assault - a costly mistake. Believing that German shellfire would prevent the lowering of landing craft, the Task Force leader decided to lower the craft twelve miles off shore. Consequently the rough weather swamped many craft and others were swept far away from their objectives, landing sea-sick soldiers in the wrong place and late. We could hear the desperate messages being passed by the troops to their parent ships during the landing process.

In order to stop the congestion caused by tanks being landed before their fore-runners had been able to clear the beach, troops on foot were landed under cover of naval destroyers going in very close with cover fire. Even Admiral Bryant took *Texas* close inshore with heavy guns blazing. Although the crew of *Bellona* were involved in bombardment duties during the landing, we were acutely aware of the plight of the American soldiers, some of whom were disembarked too far out to have a reasonable chance of reaching the beach. If they did, they could move no further forward for some time. Gradually, however, the situation improved and assault from air, land and sea swayed the battle in favour of the troops who by midnight had fought their way inland. From this point *Bellona* was engaged in two long range bombardments and some anti aircraft action before returning to Plymouth.

One of the assignments appeared to be the destruction of a water reservoir near Isigny which was carried out successfully. Many of us doubted the wisdom of such an act in an area where possession would shortly change hands and the occupying forces in addition to the French population would benefit from the reservoir's service. Perhaps we were unaware of the full facts! After a few days the troops had progressed beyond the range of the naval guns and preparations for 'Mulberry Harbour' were being made.

During this period an attempt was made by Admiral Bryant to detail our skipper, Charles Norris to call in at Plymouth to collect some Task Force mail. Regarding this as an insult to his seniority, Captain Norris asked for his position to be taken into account and a 'flash' of seniority proved him to be just about the most senior Captain in the Task Force. Each Captain was categorised by his rank and the date of appointment to that rank. U.S.S. Quincy was therefore dispatched for the mail. The outcome of this 'flash of rank' pleased Captain Norris far more than it did our crew for we would have been delighted to call into Plymouth if only for a very brief spell.

Finally, our Overlord duties complete, we returned to Plymouth where we were dispatched to Scapa Flow and joined 10th Cruiser Squadron, immediately taking part in an aircraft carrier strike against the German battleship *Tirpitz* in Alten Fiord, Norway. The effect of the strike was severely reduced owing to a defensive smoke screen eight hundred feet high. *Tirpitz,* whose life had been mainly inactive had however constituted a threat to Arctic convoys by her very presence. She was finally sunk later by RAF bombers in Tromso Fiord.

During our short time based at Scapa Flow, on one occasion *Bellona* met *Devonshire,* a County class cruiser in a boxing match. I entered the competition as the ship's heavyweight, albeit quite a few pounds of my thirteen stones plus were puppy fat. The light heavyweight and skipper of our team was Kettlewell, a Marine Corporal in his twenties and an excellent boxer. We could fit in only one training session ashore before the match. During this period 'Ketts' began to reveal some vital and alarming statistics regarding 'Nutty' Curran, the marine who he knew I would be boxing. Apparently he was eighteen stones and had boxed professionally in one or two countries where and when he was allowed to do so. As the day approached, 'Ketts' offered to stand in for me against Curran if I so wished. Tempting though the offer was I did not accept it.

On the day, the team was doing quite well. When we reached the light heavyweight bout, 'Ketts' came out at the bell, flourishing both fists in the air. His opponent cynically copied him and was immediately dumped on the canvas - and stayed there!. My turn followed - and I got my first glimpse of Curran - not a reassuring sight. He climbed into the ring stripped to the waist - thereby confirming that he was no stranger to professional boxing and stood there with two cauliflower ears. The judge immediately ordered him from the ring to don a singlet - then battle commenced. Perhaps my only achievement, albeit an unwise one, was to remain on my feet for three rounds. At the end of round one, my second, C.P.O. Stamp - our Chief Cook who was a recalled Naval Pensioner in his fifties and one time flyweight champion of the Mediterannian Fleet - attempted to boost my plummeting morale by saying to me "You've got him worried". I thought "Yes he is. Afraid of being charged with murder". During the bout, which was quite one-sided, Curran repeatedly used, and was warned about, rabbit punches. They were unnecessary for even without them he was far superior.

During the meal that followed, 'Chiefie' Stamp could not wait to inform Curran that I was only eighteen and that, in his opinion, I had fought well. 'Nutty' took all this in his stride and indicating one of his misshapen ears said to me "You hit this pretty hard early in the first round and it takes me longer to bathe it daily than it does to have a shower!" My disappointment in defeat was somewhat relieved by receiving the loser's prize of a ten shilling voucher to be spent in the ship's canteen and the generous offer of 'Ketts' to share his tot with me on the following day. To a youngster, well below twenty - the age before which nobody was allowed to draw his own tot of rum - half a cup of rum was a banquet!

At the appropriate time next day I went aft to the Marine's messdeck and joined 'Ketts' who happily congratulated me once again and handed me my 'prize'. The general atmosphere was of course one of relaxation, which only prevailed in harbour, with loud conversation as approximately sixty marines enjoyed their tots. When the noise was at its height, the door of the Padre's cabin, which was immediately adjacent, opened. Eventually there was silence then the Padre announced "Royal Marines Messdeck. I've heard nothing from you all for the last ten minutes but F --, F --, F -- and still more F --. It may well describe your last run ashore but it does nothing for me trying to prepare Sunday's sermon!". At which the Marines gave three cheers for the Padre - followed by more orderly behaviour. The ship's Padre had come across, once again, as not only a man of God, but also a man's man.

When this stay at Scapa Flow drew to a close, *Bellona* was detached once more to Plymouth Command, on this occasion to assist in keeping watch on the Biscay ports in anticipation of an enemy attempt to reinforce his forces in the Brittany Peninsular. We had not long to wait for action. Along with four Tribal Class destroyers, *Ashanti, Tartar, Iroquois* and *Haida* we attacked an enemy convoy off St. Nazaire and sank several ships including troop ships. A couple of days later we bombarded a radar station at Belle Ile. The watch on the Biscay coast was continued and on one occasion *Bellona* transferred a quantity of machine guns, ammunition, foodstuffs and cigarettes to a French trawler south of Gironde for the use of the Free French Forces of the Interior (F.F.F.I.)

A touching incident occurred during this operation. While many of our crew were at the guardrail watching the weapons being loaded on to the trawler which was below us, an old 'Stripey' noticed a young girl among the trawler's crew. With an air of disgust he shouted "What good are machine guns to her?" and quickly emerged from the canteen with a dozen bars of Lux toilet soap which he lowered down to her. Her eyes as she received them and looked upward spoke volumes. The ship received some edible crabs from the trawler in exchange for our transfer and the trawler departed with much whistle blowing.

From the outset of our sweeps off the Brittany Peninsula and Bay of Biscay, *Bellona* carried the title Senior Officer Force 26 which also included four Tribal Class destroyers. We continued to operate in the area for a further month following the operation with the French trawler.

During this period our Captain Charles Norris was understandably anxious to further his claim to a Distinguished Service Order, an award already held by many skippers of destroyers that had served or were about to serve under his command, but as yet denied him. Although a cruiser's firepower was superior to most of the enemy craft we were likely to meet in the area, conduct of the sweeps was difficult since it was always under the cover of darkness, with the relatively crude instruments of the time. Surface radar lacked the precision it now has and although it obtained initial contact satisfactorily, the speed, range and bearing provided were nowhere near accurate. Our tactics were for *Bellona* to illuminate the target with starshell once it had been detected by radar. At all times, navigation off a difficult coast swept by large tides and treacherous currents presented a hazard as did rocks and shoals together with mines laid by the enemy.

It was once said that near misses and disasters that never happened are the stuff of history but not history books. Two operations of this nature befell us to go alongside our run of successes. Force 26 was operating in darkness off the French coast when *Tartar*, one of the destroyers, reported a radar echo together with a speed which meant that the radar echo was moving and likely to indicate an enemy ship under way. Since anything mobile other than ourselves was almost certain to be the enemy, *Bellona* fired starshell over the area indicated. It quickly became evident that the 'enemy vessel' was one of the islands off the coast of France and that we had informed the German share batteries of our presence. Force 26, therefore, made for Plymouth at a speed that was not imaginary.

During the forenoon watch on the following day one of our Leading Signalmen - a joker - on duty, was wearing a small cutting from a naval collar

Ashore in Plymouth with Tony Culley to my left and Tom Carter to my right. Tom was later to become a postwar Mayor of Greenwich.

as a medal ribbon. The skipper noticed it and enquired "What on earth is that supposed to be?" Back came the reply "Battle of the Rock last night Sir!" at which he was ordered "Get below immediately and send up your relief. I'll deal with you later"

Another incident involved a minelaying operation scheduled for H.M.S. Apollo who had gone ahead to lay mines while we stood off. During proceedings, one of our destroyers picked up a radar echo far from where the *Apollo* should have been and it was therefore assumed that it was the enemy. *Bellona* fired starshell and the destroyers opened fire. Immediately a signal in fleet code was received from the *Apollo* which read "Stop. You are firing at me!" Needless to say, as we berthed at Plymouth, Apollo's crew stood at the guardrail and invited us ashore - and it was not for a pint! The reason for this misunderstanding was that the *Apollo* had decided it was not safe to lay her mines immediately and steamed well away from her original position - with all her mines still on board! Some years later I spoke to the Petty Officer Telegraphist who had been aboard the *Apollo* and he explained that it had been suggested to his skipper that he inform Force 26 of their amended temporary position. The skipper, however, quite understandably chose to maintain W/T silence (no transmissions of any kind to be made by wireless) in order not to disclose their position to enemy forces, including U boats.

Around about this time our ship's company was sadly disappointed that although technically a Home Fleet ship, the *Bellona* crew had, as yet, received no leave. This disappointment eventually took the shape of an anonymous letter slid under the skipper's door by a member of the crew. The letter contained the feelings of most members and ended with the comment "Come on Charlie, you can do better than this". Captain Norris duly cleared the lower deck forcibly expressed his opinion of writers of anonymous letters, and explained the situation as he saw it - but left his punch line for the thing that probably upset him most. It was "Worst of all, my name is Charles not Charlie!"

One incident that gave me a certain amount of satisfaction and was not without humour was a run ashore without a pay book. The naval pay/identity book had to be carried when ashore at all times and there were numerous checks to ensure that this was done. However, quite inadvertently, I left mine aboard on a bright sunny day. Having gone through the dockyard gates without detection, I realised that since I was penniless I would need to withdraw cash from my post office account. I had brought my savings book but alas no paybook for necessary identity. However, since I still wore a jumper in which my name had been sewn whilst at *St George*, that problem was surmounted.

I then became aware that my boyhood hero Joe Louis, now a Sergeant in the United States Army, was boxing an exhibition bout at a local Canadian Army Barracks, supported by many amateur contests. Not only did I gain entry without my paybook but admission was free. What a great afternoon it was. Joe and his sparring partner George Nicholson arrived in separate large cars with the Mayor of Plymouth in another. Joe invited the crowd to cheer for him as he was only a sergeant whilst George was a top sergeant. George must also have been much heavier than Joe since his back was broad enough to take the name Nicholson in very large black letters on his gown. The exhibition bout was placed in the middle of the programme surrounded by a few bouts that usually consisted of a Puerto Rican against an American. The Puerto Ricans were managing to win each bout comfortably - which did not please the Americans in the crowd - until one was matched with a black American. This bout seemed to be following the path of the others when the Puerto Rican dumped the American heavily on the canvas. As the American staggered slowly to his feet, the Puerto Rican rushed across the ring from the neutral corner straight on to a well timed and placed right jab. Good night nurse! It was the turn of the American crowd to be ecstatic. The exhibition bout was outstanding as it was a wonderful experience for me to see Joe in the flesh - boxing in my own country too!

Following the boxing I proceeded to Union Street, enjoyed a meal and rejoined my shipmates to relish telling them how much they had missed by not accompanying me during the afternoon. In the evening we attended the dance hall which was the usual venue when we managed to get ashore. There was always a great display of dancing by the many nationalities then stationed in and around Plymouth. The Americans in particular had a great line in jitterbugging and it was a common sight for the whole dance floor to be voluntarily cleared in order to watch two or three lads, with their partners, really 'cut a rug'. Before turning in we called at the local for a pint or two with a group of American GIs, mainly sergeants with whom we had become acquainted since the Normandy landings. One evening during a quiet moment, the barmaid tactfully mentioned that she hoped I wasn't going to spar up to the six feet three of the Irish American in disagreement on the colour question - again! The GIs with whom we mixed were white and considered that the black GIs should not be drinking in the same bar as them. We British sailors took a different view.

Another pleasant experience was mixing with the crew of the Polish destroyer *Blyskawica*. During one conversation a Polish sailor, the only one of our group to speak both languages, suggested that if we English had difficulty in pronouncing his ship's name, 'Bottle of whisky' would suffice. I had booked a bed with a local organisation and after a few hours slumber returned to the ship by eight o clock next morning, once again managing to conceal the absence of a paybook at the dockyard gate. I looked back on one of the most enjoyable runs ashore to date - and what was more it was done without a paybook!

Shortly before leaving Plymouth, *Bellona* played the battleship H.M.S. Rodney at rugby and we were both pleased and surprised to beat them since they carried about three times the number of crew that we did - and presumably more players from whom to select their side. It was now time to leave Plymouth since our duties connected with the ' Nazi Dunkirk' off France were complete. Nobody knew just where we were bound - except the stokers of course. They could be relied upon to spread a 'buzz'. This forecast was 'A few days leave' - if only! As we steamed north the skipper announced that we were bound for the Clyde for repairs. Could the stokers possibly be right this time? Yes they were. All hands were given five days leave, in two separate parties. As I was second leave party and had to wait five days, I spent some nights ashore with Charlie Simpson, a Radar Operator whose home was in the Partick area of Glasgow. On one occasion we travelled to Prestwick to visit his married sister. here I also met his brother, the only Bevin boy I ever met! Needless to say Charlie and I were swinging the lamp about serving in

View of aircraft carrier Nairana taken from Bellona's bridge with her 'A' turret trained for action during convoy RA64.

uniform when he was not and the hardships we considered we had to face when he said "How would you like to be shaken in the morning and have a kipper slapped in your hand immediately for breakfast?" I have never forgotten that short conversation which effectively ended there.

When the time came I spent my short leave in Brighton where my mother had joined her sister Aunt Lou to escape the bombs once again. There I was able to relax for a couple of days - to eat and drink well, sleep late and catch up with the family news rather than rely on the spasmodic arrival of mail aboard. Brother Bill was now father of a boy, Colin. Doris was mother of a boy Malcolm and expecting another baby shortly. Arthur was stationed at St. Athens, Wales. I also learned that Ron, one of dissimilar twins of Aunt Lil's, had been killed while flying a plane, on active service but not in action.

As all leaves did, this one flew and I returned to the ship to find that we had been assigned to Scapa Flow to rejoin the Tenth Cruiser Squadron. Shortly after our arrival there we took part in a night offensive sweep culminating in

Captain Tuck (right) and Communications Officer Lamb (left) on the bridge of H.M.S. Bellona during Convoy RA64.

a close range action against a coastal convoy off the Norwegian coast. This battle, and its outcome, was very similar to one of those in the Bay of Biscay. Bellona was in company with the cruiser *Kent* and destroyers *Myngs*, *Verulam*, *Zambezi* and *Alganquin*. As before, the convoy was taken by surprise and the attack pressed home from the landward side although the enemy ships were steering only two miles off the coast. The action lasted half an hour and took place between Egersund and Lister Fjord and was the first action fought by the Royal Navy within sight of the Norwegian coast for four years. The war had come full circle.

The German escorts were totally overwhelmed from the start though one put up strong resistance scoring a hit on *Verulam* before being sunk. During the action a coastal battery opened fire in support of the convoy until silenced by *Bellona*. Nine of the eleven ships were either blown up or sunk and one escort driven ashore. All our ships returned safely having suffered a small number of casualties. We then spent a further fortnight based at Scapa Flow during which time Bernard Miles came along with an ENSA group and entertained service personnel based there. This brief period of relative inactivity soon came to a close. We were to escort JW62, the next convoy, to Murmansk.

Two ratings standing beneath 'A' turret - 5.25 guns during a rare quiet period.

Convoys to Murmansk and Archangel became necessary following Hitler's failure to win the Battle of Britain and the decision to attack Soviet Russia. Shortly afterwards the 'Mission to Moscow', an entourage of high ranking officials sailed aboard HMS London bound for Russia, headed by the British Minister of Supply, Lord Beaverbrook who became known to the officers and men as the 'Beaver'. Their aim was to pave the way for Russian convoys. A leading seaman who was detailed to look after these officials was involved in an incident which when resolved, brought a smile to the faces of the ship's company. He quotes "on entering the notorious Barents Sea, conditions were bad and extremely cold and the 'Beaver', having been allocated to the Commander's cabin, found it was not warm enough for him. He had some kind of electric heater which he was trying to connect to the ship's power system. This was discovered by one of the Leading Torpedo Operators who realised that any tampering with the electrics aboard would have a dangerous effect on the degaussing equipment, thus making the ship susceptible to magnetic mines suspected to be adjacent to our track entering the White Sea. This was reported to the bridge through the usual channels". Accordingly the Leading Seaman was instructed by the Captain to escort Lord Beaverbrook to the bridge. The Captain then chastised the noble Lord in no uncertain manner. "I have over a thousand first class men in my ship's company and I will not tolerate stupidity which puts them at risk unnecessarily. We have quite enough on our hands fighting the enemy without having to play nurse-maid to His Majesty's Ministers!". Great glee spread among the lower deck on hearing the buzz that the pompous bleeder aft had been put in the 'rattle'.

As a result of the 'Mission to Moscow', there followed the immediate task of taking planes, tanks, guns, ammunition and medical supplies across the roof of the world by ships that were badly needed in other theatres of war to say nothing of the men. The escorts available for the early convoys were pitifully weak and the losses sustained once the enemy became familiar with our convoy route made it necessary for heavier escorts to be employed. Eventually the size and pattern of the convoys changed, in part to deal with the increased vulnerability to enemy U boats and aircraft. This is where the *Bellona*, a light anti aircraft cruiser came in, occupying a position in the convoy close to the aircraft carriers, with destroyers and other aircraft vessels on the screen.

On my first trip to Murmansk it was a day or two before I could think beyond the events happening aboard *Bellona*. Our traditional record to be played aboard whenever we left harbour at Scapa Flow was appropriately enough "Someone's Rocking my Dreamboat". Once the convoy had formed and each ship had taken its appointed station, a more collective picture emerged. A German reconnaissance aircraft spotted us, reported us to its Norwegian base and henceforth we would not be alone! The German occupation of Norway put us at all times within reach of enemy planes and U boats - and if they decided to take the chance - their capital ships. Many of the merchant ships, some of which were built shortly after the turn of the century, would be unable to exceed five knots before the trip was over - potentially a sitting target for U boats and planes.

On average thirty two in number, these ships would have difficulty in keeping their proper station under the prevailing conditions and in preventing the emission of excessive tell-tale smoke from their funnels. All this to a background of Arctic seas which, whipped up to a ferocity by force 7 - 12 gales for much of the run, would remain firmly in the memory of those who sailed on them. The roll of the ship would be ever present throughout each convoy - only its intensity would vary. Standing, sitting or lying could all be uncomfortable and often painful whether on or off duty. Drinking, eating and sometimes even breathing might become laborious with fittings adrift, crockery smashed, personal effects strewn about, lights out and the mess decks in various depths of water. On the upper deck objects would break adrift and would not be immediately secured. For damage control reasons hammocks would not be slung until arrival in harbour, always assuming that we did arrive. When we slept at all it would be fully clothed with (in the case of Telegraphists) the flimsy covering of a personal overcoat incapable of resisting the bitterly cold temperatures - and the inches deep sea water which would have found its way to all decks and we would be lying in it.

Despite frequent enemy action many convoy veterans would consider conditions of, and lack of opportunity to, sleep as the over riding memory of the convoys. Our ships 5.25 guns, although modest by comparison with the armament of our capital ships, were the strongest armament with which to combat enemy planes attacking the convoy. In addition the planes from our aircraft carrier would make life uncomfortable for them. Unfortunately, all too often, we were to see one of our planes returning from a successful 'dogfight' with the enemy, the pilot unable to land on his carrier because of its frightening roll caused by heavy seas. When a pilot missed his landing it usually meant a quick death. Even with the protection of flying gear, no man could guarantee surviving longer than a few minutes in winter Arctic waters. Whether or not a stranded pilot was rescued from the water depended on the proximity of U boats. At times there were twenty sailing against our convoys. On the rare occasions that none were reported in the area, a fast moving destroyer would move in with the speed of a greyhound and sweep the pilot from the sea. On other occasions the pilot was not so lucky. There was one incident on this, our first convoy, when a 'ditched' pilot still alive was spotted by members of our ship's company, many of whom were indicating to the officers on the bridge their fury that we were making no attempt to pick him up. As the Skipper explained via the ship's broadcasting system, to attempt to rescue the pilot at that time would seriously endanger the lives of our crew of six hundred.

Welcome though the sound of our anti aircraft guns was as a reassurance that we were in good hands the firing of more than one turret at a time could cause mayhem by releasing equipment that we had considered secure, around our heads. It did very little to pacify the poor ship's cat either. His behaviour seemed to border on insanity. For most of us the messdeck was a shuddering experience. However, cramped and uncomfortable the messdeck was, so often we were closed up at action stations, on duty, or asleep in water elsewhere, that 'just' an hour or two in the mess with ones messmates - and if your luck was in, a meal there - almost assumed the significance of a week's leave. When not at my action station my normal duty consisted largely of reading a continuous stream of messages from Admiralty always in naval code - our only operational link with the UK. This was done in the Central Communications Office - an office also occupied by Coders - a branch only existing in wartime.

It was usual to operate continuously in two watches (four hours on - four hours off). Sleep and reasonably prepared food were a rarity since the constant severe rolling of the ship made it physically impossible for cooks to risk cooking in the conventional manner. Consequently food warmed in tins and eaten from them was the order of the day and at regular intervals throughout the ship, tins of dry ship's biscuits were secured. Lifebelts with lights attached were worn at all times and a stout life line was rigged for those who needed to change watches on the upper deck. Mostly it was pointless, indeed impossible, to use the upper deck merely for passage from one end of the ship to the other.

Turning east, well into the Arctic Circle and north of Bear Island we were accompanied by intensified attacks from planes and U boats as well as the added risk of hitting mines laid by the Germans and which we felt at the time might well have been swept by the Russians. However when it became plain that they would not, our own minesweepers were used. Although *Tirpitz* had been recently eliminated, the enemy had replaced one threat with another by moving back to north Norway a substantial force of Junker 88 torpedo bombers. The U boat threat of course, also remained great in this theatre. In spite of this formidable strength, the enemy was unable to make any impression on this convoy which arrived unscathed at Kola Inlet. Inside the inlet, the merchantmen proceeded to Murmansk to discharge their cargoes whilst the naval vessels berthed at Polyarnoe, a small settlement usually deep in snow. A run ashore there consisted of bartering goods, usually our 'woollies' for Russian mementoes, calling in at a couple of drab shacks that passed as stores and avoiding an evil looking and foul smelling public urinal. It became abundantly clear that Murmansk was being bombed frequently by German planes from just across the border in Norway.

To the Germans, our presence at Murmansk was a guarantee that we would receive a warm reception when the returning convoy left three days later. And so it was. However the escort sailed from Polyarnoe shortly before the convoy to attack the assembled U boats during which period one was sunk by the corvette *Bamborough Castle*. A day later the destroyer *Cassandra* was torpedoed, lost her bows and returned to Murmansk for emergency repairs. Aboard *Cassandra* was Bill Culley, a stoker and brother of Cuthbert, currently in *Bellona* with me and an ex class mate of mine at *St. George*. Bill was about three years Cuthbert's senior and already had three destroyers (Js and Ks) go down under him in the Mediteranean within a period of two days. Cuthbert had not seen Bill for some years but had repeatedly claimed telepathic communication with him from time to time. Many of us were sceptical of this and teased him about it. Our attitude changed somewhat when the *Cassandra* was hit. At that precise moment, though none of the few present in his company - including Cuthbert himself - could have been aware of the incident. Cuthbert said "My brother Bill's life is in imminent danger" and went on to say that he was uncertain of his fate. The following day the corvette *Tunsberg Castle* was mined and sunk. On the same day, German torpedo bombers attacked inflicting no damage and losing two of their force. In the final days of the convoy an aircraft squadron from *Campania* sunk a U boat.

Nine days after leaving Kola Inlet the convoy reached Loch Ewe. For the escorts, a return to Scapa Flow, bleak as it was, meant a vast improvement in what may euphemistically be called life style. For the first time in almost a month we received mail from home, slept soundly in a dry, comfortable position, ate a properly prepared meal, wore warm, dry clothing, tasted a pint of beer and collected our thoughts. The run ashore at Flotta whilst the dullest in the world - Polyarno excepted - nevertheless provided comparative luxuries for the Arctic convoy sailor. They included the opportunity to see a film, maybe play some sport and hopefully perform personal ablutions with a fair degree of privacy. To walk alone was a luxury to men who for weeks had been afloat as a member of a closely quarantined community, one from which he could never escape. We had arrived back just five days before Christmas which would be *Bellona's* second successive Christmas at Scapa Flow. Shortly after our arrival Tommy Handley of ITMA fame arrived to give a show. On the day following the show, despite very rough weather in the harbour, he insisted on visiting several of the ships' companies personally. He became, unfortunately, quite unwell in the process, but his efforts to be seen by as many naval personnel as possible was both admired and appreciated by us all.

There was a five week period before we were required for a further convoy during which time the ship and its crew licked their wounds. The beer canteen at Flotta also continued to lick its wounds. It was said that sixteen replacement pianos were required in it at different times during the war and often severe drinking glass shortages necessitated crews from all ships taking pristine buckets ashore from which the lads would drink their beer - very trough like!

During this period the film 'Two girls and a sailor' was shown in our ship's canteen to different parts of the ship on separate nights. It was crammed full with leading American bands, singers and film stars of the day and portrayed the forthcoming opening of a Stage Door Canteen. In one scene, the two girls - June Allyson and Gloria De Haven - are patrolling the streets of New York attempting to entice their servicemen to attend the opening. They approached a young Texan GI walking alone, hands in pockets, towards them. "Are you going anywhere soldier?" "No Ma'am!" "Would you like to go anywhere soldier?" "Yeh Ma'am, Tokyo!" At which the whole audience erupted with incredulous cries of "You can have our bloody share!" Having already seen the film myself, if anywhere near the canteen during the subsequent showings, I could associate the time that I heard the eruptive response with that particular scene. A similar reaction greeted the sight of Errol Flynn taking Burma single handed causing the Officer of the Watch to threaten to stop the show - which I suspect would have upset nobody! Entertainment of any sort, however, soon came to an end with the sailing of Convoy JW64 - on my nineteenth birthday.

The playing of 'Someone's rocking my dreamboat" as we left harbour was more appropriate than ever. Our accompanying aircraft carriers were once again *Campania* and *Nairana*. A sighting report was made by the Luftwaffe on our second day out and thereafter almost constant contact was maintained. Later Wildcat fighters shot down a JU88 and a mass attack by forty eight torpedo bombers was foiled with the loss of seven aircraft, six to our fighters and one to *Denbigh Castle*. This was despite the lack of modern fighters in the escort carriers, with old machines operating in conditions of low light and visibility. Three days later a further torpedo attack was mounted and again repulsed, this time with the loss of seven aircraft and without damage to the convoy. Eleven U boats were deployed against the convoy and were in action three days later when *Denbigh Castle*, a corvette, was torpedoed. She was towed into Kola Inlet by the corvette *Bluebell* and a Russian tug but grounded and then capsized on arrival becoming a total loss. *Bellona* carried many of the *Denbigh Castle's* crew back to the U.K. in the return convoy. On the day before the convoy's arrival, two U boats sank the merchantmen *Horace Gray* and *Norfjell*. News was also received that the enemy were attacking the island of Soroy in north Norway. The Flag Officer detached the destroyers *Sioux*, *Zambesi*, *Zealous* and *Zest* to Soroy where they embarked the population of five hundred and brought them to Murmansk to be distributed amongst the homeward bound ships in the next convoy.

There was just one opportunity to go ashore at Polyarnoe on this occasion. The scene was as bleak as ever but brightened by one of our group on seeing a Russian female felling a tree, borrowing her axe to demonstrate how it should be done. Despite his stature of well over six feet and sixteen stone, his efforts reduced us all to panic for our safety, made no impression on the tree and had the real woodchopper creased with laughter - we thought she'd never stop! On the same evening we were given a splendid demonstration of cossack dancing by the Russian Army. It took place in a hangar aboard one of our aircraft carriers.

Two days after our arrival the return convoy left for the UK. As we did so, the corvette *Alnwick Castle* and sloop *Lark* sank a U boat. On the following morning, *Lark* was torpedoed and survivors were picked up by *Alnwick Castle* who pulled alongside. Although towed into Kola, *Lark* was regarded as a total loss. Aboard her at the time she was torpedoed were identical twin brothers Francis and Gordon Milligan, both telegraphists who had to jump for it when *Alnwick Castle* pulled alongside. (I was to meet them both fifty six years later at a North Russia Club reunion). On the same day the merchantman *Thomas Scott* was sunk by the same U boat. Another U boat hit *Bluebell* which blew up and sunk immediately. There were no survivors. The U boats had claimed three victims in one day.

× NOTE NAME MILLIGAN TWINS.

Whilst all losses of men in these horrific conditions were depressing, the sinking of *Bluebell,* stationed so very close to us was a particularly shattering experience. It all happened literally in a flash. A ship there one moment - a terrific sheet of flame - then nothing and nobody. With the weather as it was the very thought of being pitched out with the loss of one's ship in action into the screaming inferno of near freezing water did not bear thinking of - and nobody ever did think of it until it happened - and then not for long.

It was for the weather rather than the enemy's interference that this convoy was chiefly notorious and has become known, even by Arctic convoy standards as the 'great gale'. Other convoys suffered severe weather but none so bad as this. The convoy was greatly scattered with many ships suffering serious weather damage. At its height two merchant ships were reduced to steering with block and tackle on the rudder head and twelve destroyers were docked with weather damage on return to Britain. During this type of weather, our Navigating Officer, unable to take visible 'fixes' of any description used the Stavanger Beacon, to establish our ship's position - when appropriate. The beacon had been installed by the Germans and was very simply interpreted consisting, as it did, of sixty successive audible morse symbols eg: fifty dashes followed by ten dots. This allied to knowledge of the area was used to establish the ship's position. In this way the Wireless Office assisted the Navigating Officer. During the twelve days of this convoy the wind force was largely between ten and twelve on the Beaufort Scale and winds of one hundred and twenty miles per hour were experienced.

Four days out escorts had assembled all but four ships when more than twenty five aircraft attacked. Despite the weather *Nairana* flew off Wildcat fighters and they, together with *Bellona's* anti-aircraft fire accounted for several enemy planes. No ships were hit. Further hurricane winds then scattered the convoy again and it was fortunate that after reassembly, a force of enemy torpedo bombers missed the tired ships. Unfortunately they found the straggling merchantman *Henry Bacon,* one of the ships carrying passengers from SOROY Island. When the ship finally sank, some of her crew and gunners gave up their places in the boats to ensure the safety of their Norwegian guests. When destroyers found their boats all sixty five persons who had abandoned ship were still alive including nineteen Norwegian civilians but twenty six of *Henry Bacon's* crew died in the sinking. During the trip a group of official photographers took passage aboard us. I was not certain whether they were personnel from Admiralty or members of the press. Whoever they were they captured the intensity of the weather in many of their photographs and often wished themselves elsewhere. We arrived back in Scapa Flow early in March more than a little weather beaten but a coveted spell in dry dock was not to be.

Incoming mail, the first for about a month, was however as welcome as ever. My family, by now spread across the country were safe and in good health. Bill had suffered injuries whilst engaged in firefighting, especially in London's docklands. My mother remained evacuated in Brighton. Doris had evacuated to Oldham in order to give birth to her second son John, free from the bombscares. Arthur was still stationed at St Athens with the Royal Air Force. The principal war news was that the Allied troops were closing in on Berlin. We spent a month or so at Scapa Flow before sailing on our next and final convoy to Murmansk - JW66. During this time a couple of inter departmental soccer games were played ashore and I landed on each occasion to play for the Communication X1. Meanwhile one or two films were shown aboard and we all took the opportunity to catch up on sleep and general kit maintenance.

Our third convoy to Murmansk left on 7th April 1945, the escort aircraft carriers on this occasion being *Premier* and *Vindex*. Twenty seven merchantman sailed in the convoy together with a similar number of escort vessels, each of them smaller than *Bellona*. There were no incidents on passage but it became apparent that U boats were now habitually lying off the restricted access to Kola Inlet. The convoy was therefore 'blasted' into harbour with the escort steaming ahead and using all forms of anti submarine weapons in a blind barrage to discourage a patrol line of at least eleven U boats. The limitations of Asdic caused by thermal layers meant that despite the intensity of the attack, only one U boat received minor damage. The convoy however, arrived unscathed.

There was a general feeling that this war, which had been forecast by some to end by Christmas 1939 might at last just be about to end soon - approximately six years later! However the attitude of the Russians that we met had not changed. Surely the fact that our countries were only 'allies by accident' did not justify their mood of hostility and suspicion towards us. This mood was illustrated by the protection of archaic looking planes and other military equipment of their own manufacture being provided by guards with fixed bayonets to prevent our intrusion whenever we had to pass nearby. Any form of welcome was far from their minds. Their attitude did nothing to show any form of appreciation for the 'road to hell' that men had endured in order to assist them in their own superhuman efforts against the enemy. They tended to remind us of the opinion of Admiral of the Fleet, Sir Dudley Pound when the Russian Convoy plans were finalized. "The whole thing is a most unsound operation with the dice loaded against us in every direction". The return convoy left Kola Inlet on 29th April. About ten U boats were lying off the inlet waiting for the convoy but the escort groups that preceded the convoy succeeded in swamping the enemy and driving it deep during the passage. Two boats got close to the convoy, one being sunk by the frigate *Loch Shin*. Shortly afterwards the frigate *Goodall* was torpedoed. The corvette *Honeysuckle* went alongside her to embark survivors and was damaged by the explosion which finally sank *Goodall* whose officers had been aboard *Bellona* shortly before leaving Kola. She was the last naval ship to be sunk in the European Theatre of World War Two. *Honeysuckle* was later commended for her action. The next day *Loch Shin*, *Anguilla* and *Cotton* located and sank a U boat. From this point there were no further attacks on the convoy and on 8th May 1945 at 8.12am, the signal we had all been waiting for was received on BN Routines headed:

CONFIDENTIAL AND MOST IMMEDIATE - TO ALL CONCERNED HOME AND ABROAD - ADMIRALTY from Field Marshall Montgomery and received by the First Sea Lord.

Begins - As Commander in Chief of the British Empire of Western Europe I would like today to salute you and the Royal Navy.

2 - Throughout our long journey from EGYPT to the BALTIC any success achieved by the British Armies has been made possible only by the magnificent support given us by The Royal Navy with unfailing precision, we have been put ashore, supported and supplied. Our confidence has been such that the Army has never questioned the certainty of a safe landing nor of the safe arrival of our re-inforcements and supplies across the seas.

3 - I want to thank you and all those gallant sailors who have supported us with such valour. We soldiers owe the Royal Navy a great debt of gratitude and we will never forget it.

4 - Would it be possible for you to convey the gratitude of myself and those serving under me to all your Flag Officers and Captains and to all ranks and ratings of the Royal Navy. We wish the Royal Navy the best of luck.

The First Sea Lord replied as follows:

Begins - On behalf of all Officers and Men of the Royal Navy I thank you for your generous message.

2 - Ever since the summer of 1940 the Royal Navy has been eagerly looking forward to the day when we could land the Armies of the British Empire once again on the continent of Europe.

3 - We sailors never doubted that when the day came the soldiers would, however hard the struggle, achieve ultimate victory in battle.

4 - We have watched with profound admiration the progress of your operations which have now inflicted on the enemy an overwhelming and decisive defeat.

5 - Our warmest congratulations and best wishes to you and all ranks serving under your command.

This joyous news was followed later in the day by an equally popular signal from Admiralty which read 'Splice the Mainbrace', which of course meant a double measure of rum for those on the lower deck. Furthermore the convoy was informed of the national decision to celebrate victory in Europe with a two day holiday - VE Day and VE Day plus one. Each ship was encouraged to steam independently for UK and endeavour to reach a suitable port in order to join in the celebrations. We were all an appreciable distance away at the time but for the first time in months *Bellona* was able to use its maximum speed of well over 30 knots rather than one seventh of that speed, which for a variety of reasons was a common occurence in foul weather when accompanying old and weary merchant craft in convoy. The price paid for the sailing of Arctic Convoys was 21 allied warships sunk with naval casualties amounting to approximately 2,000. 98 merchant ships also suffered a similar fate with approximately 1,000 men either killed or drowned.

We aimed at Rosyth, and en route, the telegraphist that had received the joyous victory message was also very happy to receive gulpers of the C.P.O. Telegraphist's tot as a reward. Rum was issued daily to lower deck ratings over 20 years of age who agreed to it. The categories were GROG = Over 20 and drawing. TEMPERANCE = Over 20 but not wishing to draw and UNDER AGE = Not entitled. 'Sippers' and 'gulpers' of another rating's tot were usually unofficial payments for favours done - in a sense lower deck currency. Our C.P.O. Telegraphist was a man of advanced age who was called back into the Royal Navy from retirement because he had been receiving a pension from them. He was, therefore, quite relieved to hear of the end of the war and awarded the recipient of the message, an Under Age Telegraphist, accordingly.

Finally, berthed at Rosyth we were able to enjoy a decent run ashore at last - this time in Edinburgh - and enjoy the VE celebrations. We seemed to have arrived in another world. Suddenly from conditions which had tested us all to our limits we had been transferred to a beautiful Scottish city crammed with welcoming, jubilant people. I found myself one of a group of uniformed servicemen of various nationalities savouring the delights of peaceful freedom, delights which included, of course, a beer or two on the way. At one point in the day I was one of many clambering high on the statue of the Duke of Wellington mounted on horseback in Princes Street, hardly compatible with my fear of heights. Later that evening I joined a group gathered around an elderly man who was playing popular and appropriate tunes on a piano accordion. This was the first of many runs ashore in this area which included visiting Dunfermline, Inverkeithing and of course Edinburgh. One later trip to Edinburgh accentuated a sign of the times. We watched a soccer match between two Scottish First Division sides. The stadium was full and youngsters were throwing fireworks (a commodity banned during hostilities) dangerously near the visiting side's goalkeeper. Our crew felt very much at home in this area as the district of Fife had adopted *Bellona* on commissioning. Whilst the surrender of Germany was gradually 'sinking in', the immediate future of *Bellona* needed to be determined as certain current repairs were carried out. During this time it was decided to drastically reduce her complement to peace time level and as a consequence the Communications Branch would be reduced and the numbers involved in Wireless Telegraphy watchkeeping altered from thirty plus to nine.

The personnel to be drafted from the ship to Chatham Barracks were detailed. At this stage I noticed that most of my close 'oppos' were given a draft from which I was excluded so rather than stay aboard as what I regarded to be a 'blue eyed boy', I applied to be drafted to Chatham in order to sit for my Leading Telegraphist rate. This was granted and I joined the draft party in June. At this time Chatham Barracks was overflowing with matelots drafted from the ships for the same reason as we had been. Therefore an overflow camp was established at Hoo near Rochester. Since the camp began with little or no security, a surrounding fence needed to be erected before the daily rum issue could be stored. The local press wasted no time in recording this with a photograph of the contractors erecting the fence and the caption "Yo ho Hoo, and a bottle of rum". Whilst the camp was without a fence we occupants came and went much as we pleased and with my mother once again living in London, I, at last, enjoyed overnight stays at home.

The universal news suggested that the war with Japan was drawing to a close. Nearer home Hitler had committed suicide, Mussolini had been shot by his own people and hanged upside down. President Roosevelt had died, the real horror of the German concentration camps was being revealed and Naval bombardments of Tokyo had taken place. Labour had won a landslide victory in the general election - one newspaper commented 'so the nation which revered Winston Churchill as its wartime saviour rejects him for its peacetime good'. A short time after these events, the first atomic bomb was dropped on Hiroshima followed by the second of its kind on Nagasaki. I well remember hearing of the Nagasaki bomb from John Hannocks, Signalman, H.M.S. Bellona at about 5.30am one morning at Waterloo Station, as I walked on to the platform to catch the Chatham train. He had already bought a newspaper and waving it, shouted as I approached him "It's all over now". And a few days later it was. On 14th August 1945 Japan surrendered and two VJ days were announced. In the ensuing period I managed to enjoy more than my quota of V.J. days as indeed, most lads at Hoo did - aided of course by the still incomplete fence. At this stage I was enjoying the company of my mother, when at home, together with Arthur, on leave from the R.A.F. and awaiting demobilisation with twenty group as his six year service commitment had conveniently expired. A visit to Bill became a 'must' as Rose, his wife had borne a second son on VJ day! He was, appropriately enough christened Victor, and we enjoyed a moderate celebration. During September I was drafted to yet another overflow camp at Corsham, Wiltshire. It was here that I briefly met 'Cuthbert' Culley and learned from him that his brother Bill had survived the war, Cassandra having been fitted with new bows in Murmansk following torpedo damage and returned to U.K. Following 'runs ashore' in Bath I was assigned to H.M.S. Mayina a shore establishment in Colombo, Ceylon.

FAR EAST AND RETURN

On 1st October 1945 I left Southampton on the troop ship *Athlone Castle*. It was pleasant to feel the weather getting steadily warmer as we steamed south through the Bay of Biscay, the Mediterranean and the Suez Canal with groups of servicemen gathering on the upper deck in the evenings to listen to personally owned gramophones playing 78 rpm shellac records of the Andrews Sisters and other popular bands and artistes.

The mugs of tea served throughout the day were memorable both for their immense size and the fact that such an amount of steaming hot tea should have a cooling effect. As we passed through Suez Canal we noticed that the skins of the soldiers lining its banks were in sharp contrast to our white hides. To judge from their shouted remarks the fact was not lost on them either. After three weeks sailing at economic speed we arrived at Colombo and disembarked for H.M.S. Mayina, a 'stone wall frigate' carrying some two thousand five hundred matelots. One or two first impressions were quite strange to us. Firstly the language of young local children of both sex attempting to sell fruit to us through the camp boundary fence when we showed no inclination to buy. They used expletives - in English - for some time without repeating themselves. We assumed that they had learned such obscenities from our predecessors. It was also a new experience to lie back on a bunk and observe hundreds of different types of insects, large and small, encircling the light bulbs in the evening.

The standard of sport played at *Mayina* was particularly high. This was largely due to the fact that the ship's company, which in itself was large, consisted of men from many countries within the Commonwealth. They included professional sportsmen with war-time service and those awaiting demobilisation. In the Mayina International Rugby Union table, which consisted of approximately fifteen countries. England were usually trailing behind New Zealand and South Africa among others. The England versus Scotland soccer matches, were an example of the very best of skill and sportsmanship against a background of colourful and good natured support. The competition to make the Mayina 1st XV at rugby was fierce - particularly for an Englishman. I played in a trial which was organised by a New Zealander who also played for the Probables. I spent the first half propping for the Possibles. He came to me at half time and said "What's your name - Snow?" I replied "No, it's Reeve" This amused him as he realised that I had mistaken 'Snow' as his attempt to guess my name whereas it was his equivalent to mate or chum in our parlance. However, he promoted me to the Probables for the second half and I finally played two matches for *Mayina's* representative side alongside twelve New Zealanders, a South African and an Australian. What an achievement!

Whilst at *Mayina* I sat and passed my examination for Leading Telegraphist after which I was drafted to H.M.S. Sultan at Singapore. This initially involved travelling across the Island of Ceylon by train to Trincomalee on the opposite coast. The attention from insects en route caused me to scratch through the back of my battle dress top. At Trincomalee I boarded the cruiser H.M.S. Glasgow for Singapore. There I joined *Sultan,* a 'stonewall frigate' on the island of Blakang Mati.

This was my home for Christmas. Singapore was only just beginning to recover from the terrible privations of Japanese occupation and we were fortunate to receive a Christmas Day gift of two cans of Tiger Cub beer. One constant reminder of economic conditions were massive advertisements promising that Tiger Cub beer was still growing stronger. The brew before the war had been real tiger beer! Rather than queue immediately for my Christmas box, I spent the forenoon swimming in the harbour. This involved swimming out to a small vessel which appeared to have only a Japanese prisoner on the upper deck as I approached. He was leaning over the rail repeating one word in Japanese which of course I did not understand. Being a pessimist I decided that he was warning me against the risk of sharks, so rather than taking a well earned rest on the anchor cable I turned immediately and sped for the shore. Signs of the war time plight at Singapore were all around me. Possessions of military personnel of all nationalities including thousands of photographs were in evidence as were the signs of the bestial treatment given to Allied Prisoners of War at the hands of the Japanese. Changi jail was a notorious reminder. In a lighter vein, during my stay I was fortunate enough to be selected for South Malaya Rugby XV against North Malaya - an international fixture which was being resumed following hostilities and played at Kuala Lumpur. On this occasion it was notable that both teams comprised players from all three fighting services of Great Britain and its Colonies.

Before leaving *Sultan* I had an altercation with a group of Chinese workers at the ship's open air laundry. We were allowed a certain quota of garments washed free with payment required for any additional items. I considered that

I was being overcharged and left having paid what I deemed the correct price. Four workers pursued me throwing bricks. I clashed with one and bundled him into the monsoon ditch which lined the roadway. Some moments later I was struck below the eye with a brick. At this stage a group of Japanese prisoners who had arrived in a military vehicle assessed the situation, alighted to protect me and wanted to attack the Chinese, calling them 'Yellow B---s' which amusingly struck me as the pot calling the kettle yellow. However I dissuaded the Japs rather than allow them to blot their copybooks on my behalf and walked to my quarters. I was more than a little surprised when I was summoned to the Regulating Office and asked to explain why I had pitched the Chinese worker into the monsoon ditch. My embattled appearance took the Master at Arms by surprise and when he had heard my version of events and realised that the Chinese story was erroneously biased they were severely reprimanded. Nevertheless I felt a badly marked winner.

A few days later I was assigned to Naval Party 'Rat' which was bound for a Wireless Telegraphy Station at Batavia, Java. Very little was known of the duties that would lie ahead of the party as we set sail aboard a landing ship (tank). for Batavia. Unknown to us all, following the capitulation of the Japanese on 15th August 1945, the Indonesians realised that they needed to act at once if the independence from the Dutch which they had striven for since well before World War Two was to be secured. If the Dutch returned as Overlords, 'Merdeka' (the Indonesian word for freedom) may never be achieved. On 17th August a group of Indonesians forced a proclamation of Independence naming Sukarno President.

The Japs had been ordered by the Allies to maintain peace and order in Indonesia until Allied troups arrived to take control but in the face of swelling Indonesian independence, the Japanese were hopelessly ineffective. Japanese flags were downed by Indonesians publicly from government buildings and shops and houses whilst Japanese tanks were milling round the square and their planes flew overhead. They had planned to arrest Sukarno and throw him into prison. They now saw that they were too late. Millions of Indonesians were behind their new president.

Japanese flags were also downed throughout Java. They were mortified by the lowering of their flag by the Indonesians but this was nothing compared to the feeling of the Dutch colonials who expected to emerge from Japanese concentration camps and return to a luxurious life with native servants and cheap labour. Many Dutch had of course, fled the country on Japanese invasion without consulting British and American forces in Java at the time. These allied forces also became prisoners. Following the Japanese surrender the Allied forces had little or no intelligence in Java. Louis Mountbatten therefore readily heeded the Dutch Deputy Governor General Mook's false warning that the Indonesian leaders were extremist rebels and did not have the backing of the people and ordered British forces to move into Java with instructions to disarm the Japanese, crush the Republic and to return to the Dutch the properties and power they had lost three years before. The British leaders lived to regret this decision. Too late they realised that they had been manoeuvred into a false position, tricked by the Dutch.

Six weeks after the declaration of independence, British troops, some of whom had already fought in Burma, moved into Java. They were amazed to find that the Indonesians had, after a struggle, already disarmed the Japanese and placed most of them in concentration camps and the Indonesians now had the weapons that would be needed if the infant Republic was to defend its freedom. If the British were joining the cause of the Dutch, the Indonesians had to oppose them, much against their will. In the background the Dutch smiled and bided their time.

Celebrating the issue of an early tot of rum outside Communications Mess at H.M.S. Harmony at Batavia.

It was against this background that Naval Party Rat served in Tandjongh Priok, the port complex of Batavia, the Javanese capital. The party consisted largely of Communications personnel who manned the W/T station and Signal Tower both situated at the end of a dockland quay. In support of the group there was a small contingent of Royal Marines and a group of Seamen. We were based in two small separate camps immediately outside the dockyard. The question we all asked ourselves throughout our time in Java and on reflection in later life was "What exactly were we doing here?"

My own conclusion, a somewhat cynical one, was that since the Dutch were regarded as our allies during World War Two and that Britain was still to some extent Empire minded, therefore we would happily help them defend theirs. At our level, despite the difficulties of withstanding Indonesian activities we quickly found ourselves sympathising with their cause. The Dutch came across as an arrogant group and our somewhat terse description of them was 'Germans without guts'.

One regular incident which subscribed to this view was that of the Dutch Army Dockyard Sentries taking a fiendish delight in running their bayonets through sacks of grain which constituted the daily earnings of the local natives as they requested to leave the dockyard for home. It was also clear that the Dutch were landing more troops in an effort to suppress independence once and for all. The Indonesians, on the other hand, presented their own problems to us. Most were terribly poor and despite the barbed wire fences surrounding our camps they firstly entered and stole clothing left in the open to dry and finally looted our living quarters under the cover of darkness.

With 'Nobby' Clarke in our drying area where the looting came to an abrupt end.

At this stage we attempted to negotiate with them using a native policeman as a medium and interpreter to the effect that a constant armed guard would henceforth be used around the camp and that any further attempted looting would be met by gunfire. Alas! Three Indonesians were shot dead before the looting stopped.

This occurrence, necessary though it was, depressed us but was insignificant when compared with the situation further inland where British troops were closely engaged with the Indonesians in open warfare connected with the safety of personnel still in prison camps. Some were attempting to escape from them. There were many incidents of Chinese and Dutch ex internees being murdered attempting to return home. In Batavia any attempt by the Dutch to resume command in shops and properties was met by death to the Dutch.

A further hazard we faced was our colour and the fact that under certain circumstances, particularly after dark when we felt most vulnerable we could easily be taken for Dutch. The fact that the Indonesians seemed to celebrate their Independence Day each week did not help in this respect. Eventually we realised that if we had to leave our quarters in the evening other than to go on duty perhaps the beer bar was the safest place!

We felt throughout that the Indonesians had no deep desire to oppose us. They appeared to understand our position and indeed, respect us. Being British, of course, when things gradually quietened down in the area we turned to a little sport which commenced with an inter departmental soccer competition and matches against the British Army R.E.M.E. and Port Commandant teams. Eventually we endeavoured to play rugby on our home pitch and to facilitate this we merely extended the goalposts leaving the crossbars as they were. I had responsibility for organising our rugby fixtures which were generally against visiting British and Australian ships.

I could have had no idea what effect our first match was going to have on the local population. It was watched by a large crowd consisting of Japanese POW's awaiting repatriation, who were marched to all sporting events, a Ghurkha contingent, British Army personnel and several hundred Indonesians who, possibly, had never before witnessed a game of rugby. The result I do not recall but the scenes at the end of the game were tremendous - all the local natives swarmed on to the pitch throwing small objects, their own bicycles and each other into the air. We marvelled at their impression of what our game was about, albeit without a ball, and decided it was time to go - a pity in a way for they were more effective and entertaining than we had been.

With Telegraphist Reeves (a near namesake) posing aggressively towards Japanese prisoners of war in Tandjongh Priek Dockyard, Batavia.

The inter departmental soccer competition was eventually won by the Communications X1 although we were given close games by the Royal Marines and Seamen. A member of the Seamen X1 had played professionally for Fulham. I played regularly in goal for Communications and once when our sides met I got in the way of a shot of his from thirty yards. My intention was to catch the ball but it knocked me off my feet and gave the appearance that I had deliberately knocked it for a corner - for which I was applauded. Professionals do kick that much harder!

Outside Batavia W/T station with domestic staff.

Shortly before British troops left Java Louis Mountbatten paid a morale boosting visit to the island and whilst with our party presented our X1 with the League Trophy. What he had to say, from the bonnet of his jeep, seemed to suggest that our presence would not be required on the island much longer. To men who had always wondered why we were there at all, this news came as a welcome relief. An end of term feeling seemed to prevail together with availability of sporting events for those who wished to take part.

Besides being formidable soccer opponents the Royal Electrical and Mechanical Engineers Regiment lads had among their number a group of sergeants who generously opened their mess to us on several occasions and we all became good friends. An unexpected pleasure was the discovery of some baseball equipment together with a copy of game rules in a warehouse where they had been abandoned by the Americans when the Japs took command of the island. We enjoyed playing the game and challenged any visiting merchant ships that docked at Tandjongh Priok. Our view was that it was a great game when stripped of its American 'bullshine' such as "Put another pitcher on. He's a bum!"

A glance seaward from the dock area was often interesting. I once thought that I saw either of the aircraft carriers *Campania* or *Nairana* (I forget which - they were identical) entering harbour. It, however, transpired that one of them had been handed over to the Dutch Navy and renamed *Van Heemskerk* and she was arriving.

On another occasion H.M.S. Whimbrel called in and serving aboard her was Bill Duffield, a seaman - ex *Bellona*. It was good to see him again, albeit in a warmer climate. We enjoyed a few tots and a chat. Our runs ashore were invariably into the city of Batavia, some eight miles or more inland. I took part in a couple of professional boxing bouts at the Varia Stadium there, both of my opponents were Dutch. The first, Jan Zonneveld had recently arrived with the latest input of Dutch troops. The second opponent was named Hemming, an airman whose wife had been captured by the Indonesians. He believed and hoped that she was still alive. It was a worrying time for him. I managed to win both bouts and collect one hundred Dutch guilders (approximately fifteen pounds) for each win. Some weeks before we left Java, a couple of us spent a few days of long overdue leave on a local island. It was during this break that I saw, and enjoyed, my first film for more than a year - 'Rake's Progress' starring Rex Harrison, and learned a smattering of Japanese from conversations with our Japanese prisoners of war who were waiting on us. This was followed by a bout of dengue fever on my part, from which I made a satisfactory recovery. The latter fever was suffered despite taking regularly each lunchtime the issued mepacrine tablets along with lime juice, salt tablets - and now that I had reached the magical age of entitlement - a tot of rum. How much more welcome the rum would have been during the Murmansk run!

To summarise:

The British occupation of Java and the whole of Indonesia had taken place on 30th September 1945. Their task (a) to disarm and evacuate the Japanese (b) To recover the Allied Prisoners of War and internees and evacuate those so entitled (c) The maintenance of law and order within the key areas necessary for both (a) and (b) and the establishment of a civil administration (d) The introduction of food and other non warlike supplies. (a), (b) and (d) were quickly achieved but (c) proved to be an almost insoluble problem largely due to the stubborn and aggressive stand of both Dutch and Indonesians for complete control of what both countries considered to be their land.

The British finally succeeded in bringing the two parties together to negotiate a draft agreement on: (a) A proposal for the mutual reduction of military forces and (b) An arbitration clause. This was reached on 12th November 1946 but the Dutch delegate that left for Holland with the draft agreement did not return until early in 1947.

On 19th February the last of the ninety one thousand, seven hundred and ninety nine British and British Indian troops that had once been there sailed for good from Netherlands East Indies. One of the British Commander's last actions was to countermand an illegal Dutch ultimatum to the Indonesian forces. Impatient of British restraint, the Dutch army were straining at the bit. A leading Dutch newspaper in Batavia wrote 'We pray that in time, the soothing God will give us the heart and restraint to appreciate what the British have done for us" - the British who left behind five hundred of their dead.

As the world had yet to learn, this was not the end of the conflict. Following the necessity of various United Nations attempts to arbitrate, there was further military action between the Dutch and Indonesians until 2nd November 1949 following the Dutch withdrawal from Java when The Hague recognised the United States of Indonesia. The British troops, meanwhile, had left Java on 30th November 1946, including 'Naval Party Rat' from Batavia W/T some of our number for eventual demobilisation in Britain, others for Singapore, there to continue Far East service at H.M.S. Sultan.

I arrived in Singapore aboard an L.S.T. and was posted to *Sultan* on the island of Blakang Mati from whence I had left for Batavia eight months previously. Not a lot seemed to have changed in the meantime. Tiger Cub beer, according to the advertisements was 'still growing stronger'. Many servicemen were still awaiting demobilisation and much sport including rugby, soccer and water polo was being played. The whole atmosphere was such a pleasant contrast - so much more peaceful than the one I had just left in Java.

With Eddie Helps on the roof of the Fleet Administration Buildings, Hong Kong.

Outside H.M.S. Tamar (Stonewall Frigate) with four members of our rugby team prior to a match.

The economic recovery was continuing and good nourishing food was available. All of the British servicemen who had been prisoners of war of the Japanese had now been cared for and returned home as appropriate. Christmas spent at *Sultan* was very different to the one which I had experienced the year before. The centres of amusement and entertainment known as Happy World, Old World and New World had re-opened and were being widely used.

The Communications Quarters were full of personnel who had served during World War Two and there was a comfortable camaraderie amongst us. During my short stay at *Sultan* I played a couple of games of rugby and soccer, also a few games of table tennis with John Oliver, a telegraphist of about my own age who was quite an accomplished player.

Taking the sun on Victoria beach with John Oliver.

During this time my mother wrote to me reporting that one or two ex members of Party Rat who were now in Britain and demobilised had called on her on their way to their homes in the north. That cheered her up no end. Being away from her for long spells brought home to me what an excellent writer my mother was, particularly bearing in mind that she had left school at twelve years of age. Her writing was perfectly legible and her spelling immaculate. Towards the end of this stay at *Sultan* I celebrated my twenty first birthday. The large sporting fraternity to which I now belonged 'took me ashore' to Singapore city for a memorable occasion.

Early in 1947 I travelled by L.S.T. to Hong Kong W/T Station where I was to serve for the next eight months. Once again, between watchkeeping duties, I involved myself in games of rugby and soccer which were played on a vast sporting complex contained within the horse racetrack perimeter at Happy Valley. Some time was also spent sparring with Yeoman Whitfield who held the British Pacific Fleet light heavyweight boxing title. Other spells off duty were spent swimming from Victoria Beach, walking up the well known 'peak' for a commanding view of the area, jogging in the racecourse area and playing table tennis.

During my stay in Hong Kong, Princess Elizabeth married Prince Phillip which warranted a multi gun salute in the harbour. Meanwhile, sport at home included a disappointing boxing bout in which Freddie Mills lost to the American Lloyd Marshall. A very profitable event for me was the Charlton v Burnley F.A. Cup Final. As the only Londoner amongst many Burnley fans, I revelled in Charlton's one nil victory and was probably as delighted with the winning goal as its scorer Chris Duffy!

When time came for my departure from Hong Kong in November 1947 after a full commission in the Far East the ship to take me back to blighty was the minelayer H.M.S. Manxman. All hopes of being home for Christmas were shattered by the fact that, due to a corrupt delivery group, the signal instructing *Manxman* to carry out speed trials prior to an attempt on the Hong Kong to U.K. time record was wrongly routed. Consequently *Manxman,* a ship capable of a speed twice as fast, proceeded throughout at the economic speed of fifteen knots. A further delay occurred when we needed to call in at Aden because of a local conflict there.

The New Year was 'seen in' at Gibraltar where I was involved ashore in a bar fracas between a contingent of the French fleet and one of our own. It was broken up by the Military Police, who, to me, appeared to remove all members of my group except myself. My somewhat inebriated mind took exception to this and I somehow staggered my way to the local police station in an attempt to rejoin my shipmates. Outside the station, two Military Police, one Army and one R.A.F. assured me that whatever I did, it would be impossible to join my friends. I quickly proved them wrong by going to the roadside and urinating over the bonnet of a car which, unknown to me, was the property of the Chief of Gibraltar Police. My feet barely touched the deck as I was taken inside to join my shipmates. We all spent most of the night in custody but were released during early morning as the Skipper had informed the shore authorities that he was sailing shortly.

Later in the day, as *Manxman* turned the corner into the Bay of Biscay, I, among many others, appeared individually before the Skipper at his 'defaulters' parade. He proved to have a lively sense of humour - he also very quickly got to the point."Where do you live in the UK Reeve?". "Dulwich, London, Sir". "Tell me - do you go p---ing all over the streets of Dulwich?" "No sir. There is no shortage of public toilets in Dulwich!" "You received ample warning that there was a shortage of them in Gibráltar, before going ashore didn't you?" "Yes sir" "Furthermore, how could you fail to recognise the Chief of Police's car with his pennant flying on the bonnet is beyond me - two days stoppage of leave, starting today!" "Yes sir" - On cap and away. The subtlety of the punishment showed kindness on his part for we were to take two days to reach Sheerness! We did so early in January and two things quickly occurred, one favourable, the other definitely not so. Firstly, the organiser of R.N. Chatham and Nore Command Rugby Club who was also a representative on the committee forming a new United Services Chatham Club came aboard to see me and offer me a playing position in both outfits.

The less attractive matter was that the crew of the *Manxman* were to take their leave entitlement in two separate groups. This was a normal procedure, but the fact that I was in the second group did not please me as I had served in the Far East approximately twice as long as the ship's crew and was also entitled to a much longer uninterrupted leave. As I had been technically taking passage home - albeit one during which I worked - and would be clearly be receiving a draft elsewhere before very long I was disappointed and informed the Master at Arms as much. This got me nowhere and matters did not improve when I took advantage of all night leave granted to many of us on our first night in harbour to visit my mother in London and failed to return by eight o clock the next morning. I spent the following month or so aboard *Manxman*. She required a refit and during this time I was able to pay short visits home and represent Nore Command and United Services, Chatham - whose home ground was in Gillingham. My brother Arthur had by now been 'demobbed' for some time. He had also been ill. The asthma which had plagued him all his life had for much of my absence caused him to be seriously affected.

The drop in temperature of a British winter following my time in the Pacific, much of it on or near the equator, led me to spend most of my time in an overcoat, even at meals. How lucky I was not to have returned home during the previous year - 1947 - when Britons struggled in the grip of one of the worst winters ever recorded, combined with a serious fuel shortage which brought the country to its economic knees.

It was quite clear that a much greater variety of good food and other commodities had been available in the Far East than at home where rationing was still in force, and in some cases had recently been reduced in amount. Whilst in the past I had sent home kippers from the Isle of Man and tea from Ceylon, I had no idea when returning home that necessities and luxuries were in extremely short supply. This was in some measure due to my mother's stoicism when writing to me. However I was reasonably laden with 'UK unobtainables' on my return - something for each member of the family including some fine denier stockings for my sister who in my absence abroad had been treated for tuberculosis, finally convalescing in Ventnor, Isle of Wight.

It was not until my turn for long leave came that I had a couple of months to look around me and really feel at home. I was able to visit members of my family at leisure and the families of ex shipmates and other servicemen who were still in the Far East. But something was missing. Other than my own family, I now knew fewer people with whom I could spend time during the day than when I had left the country three years previously. For one thing, my mother was living in yet another area, furthermore, anybody remotely near my age was working.

When my leave expired, I was drafted to Nore W/T Station at Chatham. This was a station in touch with the Admiralty at Whitehall and keeping a Port Wave open for ships in the Nore Area, watches were worked forty eight hours about and all time off was spent either in the Medway area, or when forty eight hours off at home in London. This gave me an excellent opportunity to attend the Olympic Games which were held in London. Two Olympics had been abandoned after Hitler's 1936 Nazi propaganda spectacular in Berlin. These London Olympics were held among the strictures of post-war austerity, and proved to be inexpensive, unpretentious but successful. Without the resources to build new stadiums, the organisers used traditional venues but Wembley with a new cinder track in the stadium and the Empire Pool nearby were the main focus. It was to Wembley that I travelled as often as possible with the odd cycling visit to watch Reg Harris gain the silver medal for Britain in the 1,000 metres sprint.

The athletics performances that impressed me were those of Arthur Wint (Jamaica) who won the 400 metres, was second in the 800 metres but had the frustration of retiring with cramp during his leg of the 4 x 400 metres relay. Emile Zatopek (Czechoslovakia) who won the 10,000 metres and was a very close second in the 5,000 metres - but perhaps most memorable were the achievements of Fanny Blankers-Koen, a Dutch housewife and mother who arrived as World record holder in both high and long jumps. She competed in neither and, instead, won four track events - 100 and 200 metres, 80 metres hurdles and 4 x 100 metres relay. She, like myself, needed public transport to attend the stadium- a post war Olympic village was yet a dream!

In addition to the track athletics at Wembley, I watched boxing and Greco Roman wrestling in the pool area. The commissionaires at the entrance to these events invariably and very kindly allowed me in for all three sessions per day for the price of the morning session only. Perhaps my naval uniform had something to do with it!

I continued to play rugby for Nore Command and U.S. Chatham. During this time we suggested to Blackheath R.F.C. that as we were handsomely beating their Second XV whenever we met we should be given a fixture with their first side. Their cold reply was "No. There is only room for one first class side in Kent!" Perhaps they considered that being the oldest club in the world entitled them to speak in such a way. However our Secretary gave them the V sign and obtained a fixture with Coventry, one of the strongest sides in the country at that time and both clubs enjoyed the new fixture. For our part, we were challenged to give our very best performance to 'live' with them and Coventry clearly enjoyed the company of men from all three services - especially after the match.

During 1949 I was posted to H.M.S. Steepholm as its only wireless operator. *Steepholm* was an ex-minesweeper, now on wreck dispersal duty with sister ships *Flatholm* and *Tiree*. This involved clearing the east coastal sea bed of the many vessels sunk during the recent war which were a danger to navigation. We operated from Sheerness, Lowestoft, Felixstowe and Grimsby and were a happy crew as small crews are likely to be because they are so closely knit.

One of our operations which attracted the attention of both the Admiralty and the population of Lowestoft was the dispersal of a wreck near the Suffolk coast. Within a short time of our beginning to explode depth charges, the Admiralty were in touch with us enquiring as to the power of charges which we were exploding. The reason for the enquiry was that alarming cracks were appearing in the ceiling of the local police station. Fortunately we were able to report that we were using no more than the minimum effective charge - which satisfied Their Lords! The big reception was still to come and took place when we attended an 'at home' at an R.A.F. establishment near the scene of the crime. Many of the population turned out to congratulate us on 'sinking' the police station.

We had aboard us an Able Seaman Pratt, who during the war had acquired an extremely nervous disposition. One day our skipper decided that the ship's company needed a reminder on initiative. He mustered us all on the upper deck and during the lecture got a little over enthusiastic. Throwing his cap onto the deck he shouted "That's an incendiary bomb. What do you do with it?" Dickie Pratt, giving his familiar high pitched giggle, stepped smartly forward saying 'I'll show you what to do with it" and threw the cap over the side into the water. We took the fact that Dickie was not punished to mean that the Skipper was favourably impressed with his reaction!

My representative games with the United Services at rugby continued throughout my service aboard *Steepholm* and often necessitated my being landed in the early hours of Saturday morning in order to reach the appropriate ground in good time for kick off, and with the game played enjoy the remainder of the weekend at home. After a year or so aboard *Steepholm* I was drafted once again to Nore W/T and later affected by a Queen's Order in Council which meant that several branches of the service, the Communications Branch included, were required to serve a further eighteen months. This was due to the outbreak of the Korean War.

I, however, remained at home and continued to play for United Services at rugby. Following a successful Easter tour in Wales, we were playing against Old Alleynians on Dulwich Common quite close to my home. Long before the game ended a dense fog had descended. A team mate Harry Course, who lived in the Midlands, was depending on me to escort him to an Euston bound tram that evening. What would normally have been a simple walk of a few minutes duration took much longer and resulted in my passing my own house without realising it at the time before dispatching Harry.

Simultaneously, something far more serious was occurring to my sister, Doris, not too many miles away in Wallington. Having already been treated for tuberculosis for many years, she had been mobile for only a few days when she shopped locally on this particularly foggy Saturday. This was sufficient to add pleurisy to her ailments from which she soon died - at the age of thirty seven. As she had neither drunk alcohol nor smoked and as the only drugs she had taken were those with which the medical profession were striving to make a breakthrough in tuberculosis treatment, there seemed to

Sister Doris with her two sons Malcolm and John in their back garden in Wallington, Surrey.

me little justice in the world at this time and it was difficult for me to believe that her death was the will of God. Worse still, she had left Fred and two sons, Malcolm, nine and John seven. I reasoned hard with my Senior Officer at Nore W/T to be allowed leave not only to attend the funeral but to stay with Fred to support him leading up to it. In this I was successful. The cremation of Doris was the first service of its kind that I had attended and the sudden dissapearance of her coffin behind a curtained screen seemed both sudden and final - something for which I was not prepared. I felt like reaching out to touch it.

Two submarine disasters took place during my final home fleet commission. In 1950 HM Submarine Truculent was rammed by a Swedish merchant ship in the Thames Estuary. There were some survivors but an ex *St George* shipmate of mine Tom (Scouse) Edwards was not among them. I had last seen Tom in 1943, when he was serving aboard the battleship *Duke of York* which took part in the action in which the German battleship *Scharnhorst* was sunk - and was anticipating some leave. In May 1951, H.M. Submarine Affray was sunk with all hands. Aboard her was another ex *St George* shipmate, Irvine, whose Christian name I do not recall. Ironically, they both survived the war only to die at sea in peacetime.

My time for discharge duly arrived in 1952 but my final medical examination in Chatham Barracks revealed that I was suffering from hepatitis which meant spending a few weeks in the Naval Hospital at Gillingham. I was in notable company since both Prince Philip and Anthony Eden were stricken with the same complaint at the same time. The former, however made me quite envious by shaking off his bout within a couple of weeks and in time to attend the Olympic Games in Helsinki while I lingered for many a week on senna pods and a fat free diet with Kay Starr singing 'The wheel of fortune' in the background. What beastly luck!

Finally I was discharged and collected my 'demob' suit at Woking, descending upon 'Civvy Street' as an adult for the first time in my life.

LET'S HAVE A LITTLE BIT MORE

Choosing a career ashore after ten years in the Royal Navy presented some difficulties. There were no rehabilitation courses available and the choice seemed to be between pursuing wireless telegraphy - the only trade I knew, and striking out into an entirely new field. The Post Office were welcoming ex Naval Telegraphists and paying one tenth above the basic rate for overnight shifts. Paltry though this seemed, it was, after all, one tenth higher than I had been receiving in R. N. for night watches! These were the days when service pay was a very poor relation to civilian pay. However I made an early decision that I would dispense with night watches altogether and for the first time in many years sleep all night every night. In addition I would value my labour rather than amass a great number of hours work weekly in order to exist.

The first aim was easily and immediately fulfilled. The second required a few years continuous effort and entailed acquiring a professional qualification. I was still due a few weeks leave on discharge but such was my enthusiasm to tackle Civvy Street that I applied for a post with Port of London Authotriy and following an interview and swim test - of all things - began work a week or so after leaving Royal Navy.

My first duty was in Surrey Commercial Dock Timber Section, as a Customs Clearing Assistant, a post which included an office very close to that of the Area Timber Inspector. It was here that I was soon to learn that self discipline and respect for authority were virtually non existent and the sight of a docker, dissatisfied with his previous days bonus, bursting in on the Area Inspector without knocking at the door and completely unannounced was commonplace. After Royal Naval discipline this was, indeed, a revelation to me.

Shortly after joining P.L.A. I was engaged as a Timber Measurer which involved computing the dimensions of hardwood with the aid of a slide rule and working at sufficient speed to enable the attendant gang of four dockers who handled, craned and stowed the timber to earn a respectable piece work bonus per day. The conflict between their rate of progress and my adherence to administrative requirements, including those of safety, was ever present and provided me with an important area of decision making in carrying out my duties. Whilst it was customary for each 'ganger' to collect a donation from each member of his gang at the end of the week, as a reward for his measurer (who was not on piece work). It was by no means unknown for 'gangers' to burst into the office to query their previous days bonus when it became known. One particular 'ganger' I occasionally worked with, delighted in choosing the busiest time of the day to visit the Foreman's Office in order to query the gang's previous day's bonus. One day he omitted to do so - so I said to him sarcastically "Isn't it time to go and dispute your bonus?" He replied "I have no query today". When I suggested that he should go to the office and query why there was no query he did not share his gang's delight at my remark.

The piece time rates still being paid to dockers as late as 1952 when sophisticated machinery was available were based, in some instances, on handling each piece of timber separately throughout as had been necessary during the pre-crane era. However, they felt justified in going on strikes regularly. Little wonder that they priced themselves out of the international commercial market!

On leaving the Royal Navy, I had joined Saracens Rugby Club but since conditions with P.L.A. allowed only six Saturday mornings off per year, it was extremely difficult to do justice to a fixture list which included many long distance away games. Consequently, after a season with Saracens I joined P.L.A. Rugby Club whose home ground and clubhouse was at Redbridge, Essex, and wbose away fixtures were somewhat nearer than had been the case with Saracens. My journey to Redbridge involved a trip right across London, south to north, and often further for away fixtures. This journey was initially made by tube train, the arrangement being superseded by travelling in a vintage (1932) car owned by Mick Morris who lived near to me in Dulwich. Eventually following the recruitment of John Mather - an ex prisoner of war and fellow P.L.A. employee - to the club, I found myself riding pillion aboard his 1.000cc Vincent motor cycle with two sets of rugby gear across my back.

One Saturday afternoon following a match against Old Blues at Fairlop, John and I were enjoying a post match pint when he raised my blood pressure by informing me that we had been 'doing a ton up' (100 mph) on our way to the match. This was a regular occurrence but as he related it I spotted on the other side of the bar William Hartnell - television's first 'Doctor Who' and an actor who had appeared in many cinema film and stage shows and whom I had recently seen with Ronald Shiner in 'Seagulls over Sorrento'. John disagreed as to his identity so, following a small wager, we trotted over to join him. It proved to be William who was also an Old Blue and was performing in 'Seagulls' later that evening. When we showed surprise that he was relaxing with a drink many miles from the theatre on the evening of a performance he smiled and said that he knew his lines backwards and would have no problem later on stage.

John and I were therefore, able to exchange one shock for another - his mention of the 'ton up' and my winning the William Hartnell wager! My rugby experience with P.L.A. lasted from 1953 until 1959 during which time I captained the club including a representative match against Combined Shipping Companies and represented Eastern Counties and Essex. The club also took part in a few Easter Rugby Festivals in Bournemouth and Lowestoft. Whilst at the Lowestoft Festival we used a hotel in Great Yarmouth which was owned and run by the Paishley family, whose daughter Ann was an international sprinter and an outstanding vocalist. One of our wing threequarters, having imbibed freely one evening made the mistake of challenging her to a sprint along the sea front. He came a poor second!

During 1956 I developed a duodonal ulcer - one without the usual post meal pain which resulted in me being quite oblivious of its existence until I fainted on the altar at my brother Arthur's wedding, acting as his best man. This occurred on a Saturday when I would usually have been playing rugby! Mother was on hand with the smelling salts and I continued with my role. In my reception speech I attributed the incident to shock at my brother finally marrying - at the tender age of 43! In fact the faint was due to a haemorrhage which took place following the bursting of the ulcer during the wedding ceremony. The results of a medical examination on the following Monday began a dull and uninteresting period during which time I was confined to bed and required to follow an equally dull and uninteresting diet. The only bright spot of the confinement was to hear Chris Brasher winning his gold medal in the Olympic Games Steeplechase at Melbourne. When eventually mobile I was required to receive injections to increase my blood count as iron tablets were not producing satisfactory results. My doctor seemed to enjoy emphasising the great cost of these injections to the National Health Service. Since this was my first call on a practitioner since leaving R.N. four years previously I could perhaps have been forgiven for considering that as the nation had had my blood when it needed it, it would not mind replacing some in my hour of need.

Following eventual recovery I left Port of London to join the Housing Department of London County Council. Two years later I joined the Electricity Supply industry at Lewes District of South Eastern Board. In 1963 I was promoted to an Administrative post in Croydon district where I qualified as a Chartered Secretary and in 1969 was further promoted to Executive Officer (Personnel) at Manchester Area of North West Electricity Board, taking early retirement in 1983 having served a total of twenty four years in the Electricity Supply Industry. I agreed to early retirement for a variety of reasons which included compiling a list of interests containing as many of an active nature as those that were sedentary. It was an additional incentive that during fourteen years with NORWEB I had attended approximately fifty funerals in my capacity as Personnel Officer.

I have enjoyed several hobbies since my naval days, the most durable - and one already referred to being the continuation of playing and coaching Rugby Union in which I was involved for a total of fifty six seasons. During this time I represented three counties - Eastern Counties, Essex and Sussex and several clubs including United Services Chatham, Saracens, P. L. A., Seaford, Eastbourne and Shirley Wanderers - two of which I skippered.

Seaford 1st XV which I skippered during season 1960 - 61

During my time with Eastbourne, the club provided a 'home' for a week or so to All Blacks, Wallabies and Springboks touring sides as and when appropriate. This arrangement was convenient for them as their first fixture was against Southern Counties at Hove. We also provided similar facilities for

The author joining a break through a United Banks line out - Sussex v United Banks, 1962

outgoing British Lions sides, on one memorable occasion combining our own Annual Dinner with a farewell Dinner for them. On one tour Willie John McBride, who had badly injured a foot during the domestic season was informed that with continuing treatment he might be fit for the final tests in South Africa. Meanwhile he took part in line-out practice wearing one boot and one soft shoe. As for the incoming touring sides, two of them presented a very different front. The All Blacks were most friendly and it was a pleasure for me to witness my young daughter Sally, and young son Adrian sat on the lap of Don Clarke, the outstanding full back of those times, during an informal training session. During another tour, however, the Springboks were quite difficult to entertain and invariably occupied one end of our bar whilst we occupied the other. At this stage of the tour we readily accepted the fault to be with ourselves, since we were the host club. As the Springbok tour advanced, however, it became clear, even at International level that they were difficult to get alongside particularly when their discussions were in Afrikaans.

Whilst playing for Shirley Wanderers I took a side to Twickenham R.F.C. and prior to the match, as I passed the opposing team's changing room with door ajar, I was inexplicably drawn towards a player standing inside. I had no idea why or what I would say when I reached him. However I managed to say something like "I think you may be my cousin and if so your name is either Len or Wilf". He said "I'm Len, but who the hell are you?" When I replied we both acknowledged how extraordinary it was that I should recognise him thirty years after we had last met - as young boys - playing in my Uncle Bill's

Shirley Wanderers 2nd XV skippered by the author during season 1964 - 65

garden at Richmond. Needless to say we enjoyed the evening during which it became evident that we had both served in Royal Navy during WW2. The incident also resulted in my reunion with my mother's side of the family.

In more recent years I joined Manchester Rugby Club and became a founder member of the Evergreens of Rugby (EGOR) - the first club to register with the English Rugby Football Union to play over 40s rugby. My foreign tours have included those to Australia, New Zealand, Canada, Portugal, Germany, Spain and Ireland.

Line out close up during a game between Manchester Over 40's (which I skippered on the day) and EGOR (The Evergreens of Rugby). The author is caught exchanging pleasantries with his opposite number Jack Barrett. Also in camera are Manchester players Ted Bonner, Wyn Jenkins, Gordon Smith and Keith Phillips whilst Roy Welch and George Juniper are members of the opposition.

A quartet of EGOR 'Oldies' who played in the London Festival of Golden Oldies during the 1980's. Left to right are Bill Haynes, Harry Scott (who played for England against France at Twickenham in 1955), John Dewhurst and the author. White shorts (John) signified over 40, black (Harry) - over 50 and red (Bill and the author) over 60!

Another pursuit which attracted me, although only for a short time was open water swimming. This came about when I chose to discover how far I could swim uninterrupted by the end of a swimming pool. I joined Warrington Dolphins, a member club of the Long Distance Swimming Association, Whilst with them, together with other minor achievements, I swam Lake Coniston in an August temperature of $58^{o}F$! I also tried my hand, very briefly, at Korfball, a game of Dutch origin which when I played it was, to the best of my knowledge, only practised to a minor degree in this country - in the South and in the Rotherham area.

During 2001 I joined Thorn Grove Bowling Club, Cheadle Hulme. Whilst still decidedly on a learning curve I thoroughly enjoy the crown green game and the camaraderie that accompanies it. Allotment vegetable growing entered my life thirty years ago and despite the fact that all my children have 'flown the nest', I continue to grow as much as ever. How long my energy will hold out, however, remains to be seen. Public speaking occupied some of my time for a few years during which period I was elected President of Stockport Speakers Club which is a member of the National Association of Speakers Clubs. During my time there I won competitions at Club, District and Area level and on one occasion reached the National Evaluation Final. More recently I still give light hearted talks to various organisations, particularly those where members are unable, for whatever reason, to travel for entertainment.

Speakers Club evaluation trophies won in season 1988 - 89 which include those for competitions at Area and District level and gavel and block for participation at National level.

Membership of Poynton Male Voice Choir for a few years was most enjoyable and a busy time. The choir produced many concerts per year, possessed an efficient, hard working choirmaster, lady pianist, and committee - together with an extremely friendly atmosphere. As an indoor interest, philately has ranked high on my list. Although I have now virtually ceased adding to my collection for many years I enjoyed collecting the stamps of Great Britain.

Happy band of shipmates and wives at an early H.M.S. Bellona reunion.

In recent years Naval Reunions have, happily, taken up some of my time. Firstly, in 1980, I became aware of a H.M.S. Bellona reunion which had just begun as an annual event and was being held in London. I contacted the organiser Arthur Willis and attended regularly until a few years ago when they were discontinued. During this period I was reunited with several of the Ship's Communication Branch, all of whom I remembered and knew well. Since I lived two hundred miles from the various reunion venues, I accepted the thoughtful invitation of Arthur and Lila, his wife, to stay at their Shepperton home at the time of these reunions.

The North Russia Club is another organisation to which I belong. Its members consist of those who served on convoys to Murmansk and Archangel, Naval Parties stationed ashore in that area and some RAF personnel. Annual week-

The author receiving a commemorative medal from a Russian Army Officer at the Russian Embassy.

end reunions are still organised - the one in 2003 being at Weston Super Mare. We have our own magazine 'Northern Light'. During 1985 U.S.S.R. awarded a medal to appropriate servicemen who had served on Arctic Convoys, the inscription on the dedication read 'To those who served in the Great Patriotic War against Fascism 1941 - 45 - 40th Anniversary of Victory' The Russians did not recognise World War 2 as such. Following our receipt of the medal at the Russian Embassy, Kensington Gardens, NRC were invited to visit Murmansk, Leningrad and Moscow for Russia's Victory Week Celebrations. Our members and wives made the journey during that region's few annual days of summer. The previous warning to take very warm clothing on the trip eventually caused much mirth among the ladies who swiftly began to doubt their menfolk's description of the weather in North Russia. On this visit the skies were clear throughout with daylight until well past midnight, and the schoolboys at Murmansk were allowed to abandon other lessons in order to play football as this was impossible for most of the year. One or two of our group were crazy enough to join them. We were treated extremely well throughout the tour - even as heroes! This splendid heartfelt reception which we received contrasted favourably with the indifference shown us in the 'dark days'.

In 1994 veterans of a dozen allied naval ships engaged off the French coast during the months following the Normandy landings in 1944, were invited by French historians to the town of Bretignolles Sur Mer for five days. The stay included a comprehensive celebration of the success which these ships had achieved during August 1944. This success was won by three naval forces (Nos 26, 27 and 28) each comprising a cruiser and destroyers sinking many German naval ships and troop carriers off the west coast of France. One such force was H.M.S. Bellona (S.O. Force 26) accompanied by the destroyers H.M.S. Tartar, H.M.S. Ashanti, H.M.C.S. Iroquois and H.M.C.S. Haida who sank six ships sailing from St. Nazaire in darkness on 5th August 1944.

Veterans together with the Mayor on the coast at Bretignolles.

Four ex-*Bellona* crew, including myself, made the trip together with sixteen other veterans and we were all billeted with French families in Bretignolles. During our stay we were welcomed by the Mayor, attended an exhibition of Bay of Biscay battles, participated in various debates with historians and were generously feted at functions. On the final day we attended the inauguration of a commemorative plaque in honour of those who died in action.

At one of the debates held in a large hall, we twenty veterans were asked to take the stage, introduced to an audience of five hundred people and then requested to give our individual account of our particular part in the action

Shipmate Arthur Willis and the author together with Lyonce our Bretignolles hostess.

which had occurred fifty years before. When my turn came, rather than repeat much of what had already been said, I chose to relate a relevant incident which had made an everlasting impression on me. It concerned the process of transferring firearms and ammunition to a French trawler south of Gironde for the use of 'Free French Forces of the Interior. 'Stripey' looking down at the trawler's deck and spotting the only female aboard bought a supply of Lux toilet soap at the canteen and lowered it to her. How delighted she was. As I stepped from the stage, a lady and gentleman approached me. The gentleman who spoke good English, congratulated me on my talk and introduced the lady as the only female member of the trawler crew in 1944. It's a small world!

At the Commemorative Plaque Inauguration on the final day, three delegates including the Mayor of Bretignolles, made speeches to a crowd of many hundreds. The speeches were, of course, all in French. I, however, had a personal interpreter (the gentleman who had met me after my talk the previous day). When the Mayor was in full flow, my interpreter nudged me in the ribs and with a smile said "He is now telling them about the toilet soap". By then the whole crowd was smiling! The memorable occasion was one of many during our stay. The initial invitation by the historians and population of Bretignolles had been a complete surprise to all veterans involved and like many surprises of its kind was a very pleasant one.

My first marriage, soon after leaving Royal Navy gave me my first son, Roger. My second marriage some years later, to Barbara, provided me with a daughter Sally and three further sons, Adrian, Richard and James. Since 1969 we have lived in Cheadle Hulme, Cheshire. Barbara and I have now been together for over forty eight years and enjoy this area of the country and in particular the northern hospitality. We are thankful that we remain in reasonable health and thoroughly enjoy our time together in addition to that spent with our family and grandchildren.

A family photo taken at a farewell get together for Richard, Bianca and Baby Myles. Left to right: Back row - Richard, Bianca, Myles on knee, Charles, Alice and David. Middle row - Lisa, James, Sally and Barbara. Front row - Susan, Harry, Adrian with Jessica in arms. Alice and Harry are Sally and David's children. Two further arrivals since the photograph was taken are Eric, son of Adrian and Susan - and Anabel, daughter of Richard and Bianca.

The author making them have 'a little bit more'.